A Grim Almanac of
York

A Grim Almanac of
York

Alan Sharp

First published 2015
Reprinted 2019

The History Press
The Mill, Brimscombe Port
Stroud, Gloucestershire, GL5 2QG
www.thehistorypress.co.uk

© Alan Sharp, 2015

The right of Alan Sharp to be identified as the Author
of this work has been asserted in accordance with the
Copyright, Designs and Patents Act 1988.

All rights reserved. No part of this book may be reprinted
or reproduced or utilised in any form or by any electronic,
mechanical or other means, now known or hereafter invented,
including photocopying and recording, or in any information
storage or retrieval system, without the permission in writing
from the Publishers.

British Library Cataloguing in Publication Data.
A catalogue record for this book is available from the British Library.

ISBN 978 0 7509 6063 2

Typesetting and origination by The History Press
Printed by TJ International Limited, Padstow, Cornwall.

CONTENTS

ACKNOWLEDGEMENTS	7
INTRODUCTION	9
JANUARY	11
FEBRUARY	25
MARCH	39
APRIL	55
MAY	73
JUNE	85
JULY	99
AUGUST	117
SEPTEMBER	133
OCTOBER	149
NOVEMBER	161
DECEMBER	175
ABOUT THE AUTHOR	189
BIBLIOGRAPHY	190

St Mary's Abbey, York. (© Allan Harris)

ACKNOWLEDGEMENTS

Although the author's name is the one that appears on the cover of a book, in reality, writing a book is always a collaborative experience. I would like to give my thanks to everyone who has helped me along the way, in whatever capacity.

In particular, I would like to thank the staff of the York Explore Library, where I spent long hours finding the accounts that appear within this book. They are ever helpful and patient, and without the wonderful resources they provide, this book would not have been possible. Also, the staff at the York Museums Trust, York Minster and the Minster Library, and the Jorvik Group.

Thanks also to the individuals who have helped either with information or with sourcing illustrations. These include Karen Adams, John Cooper (University of York), Darren Flinders, Allan Harris, and others who have given a word of advice here and there. All uncredited images are property of The History Press.

Finally, on a personal note I would like to thank my family and friends for putting up with me; the guides who have worked with me at White Rose York Tours during this period and who have helped make that company a success which, in turn, has helped me to learn so much more about this fantastic city; Laura over there in the States, who will always sit patiently on the end of a phone and allow me to vent about anything that's on my mind; Matilda Richards at The History Press for giving me the chance to write this book; and anyone else I may have forgotten that helped me along the way.

York skyline overlooking St Mary's church and the minster. (Author's collection)

INTRODUCTION

York. The capital of the North.

From its foundation in AD 71, York has always been at the heart of the United Kingdom. The Romans built the first defensive camp here, and made it the administrative centre of their northernmost province. The Anglo-Saxon kings of Northumbria made it their capital, and the Vikings ruled over vast swathes of English soil from within its defences. William the Conqueror came here, capturing the city to consolidate his power in the North, and Henry III lived within its walls and turned it into a veritable stronghold.

York was the northern staging post of the Plantagenet kings as they attempted to win Scotland and bring it into the realm. The bloodiest fighting of the Wars of the Roses raged in the countryside just beyond the walls, while the heads of noblemen stared lifelessly from spikes atop the city gates. Henry VIII came here during the Reformation and changed the city irrevocably. And its besieging and eventual capitulation was one of the major turning points of the English Civil War.

And while the vast canvas of history was painted large across the city, smaller stories were told quietly in the background. At the Knavesmire and in the grounds of York Castle, the hangman plied his trade dispatching murderers, rapists and common thieves as well as the highwaymen who terrorised the roads north from London. Famous criminals like Dick Turpin and William 'Swift Nick' Nevison found themselves dangling from the York gallows tree, alongside men whose names have been forgotten to history, although their crimes were no less heinous.

And then there were those less deserving of their fate: Catholic priests and recusants whose only crime was to worship their God in their own way and not the way that kings and queens had chosen for them; noblemen who had chosen the wrong side in some petty squabble between the great families, where – had things taken a different turn – they might have been hailed as heroes instead of having their heads separated from their bodies.

Come with me, down past the Knavesmire, to the Micklegate Bar, where the young King Edward IV rode into the city in glory having secured the throne for himself and for the House of York. It was along this way that St William rode also, on his triumphant return to the city, not yet a saint but about to meet the destiny that would raise him up to that hallowed position. Here, in this affluent quarter of the city, they would have passed the houses of the good and great, the rich merchants and businessmen, as they rode down to the Ouse Bridge, then the only crossing of the river other than by ferry.

So on to the bridge itself, standing in this spot since the time of the Vikings, although the Romans had built their own river crossing not 300 yards distant. This bridge, the lifeline holding the two sides of the city together, was once covered in buildings, including a prison and England's first public convenience built in one of the arches in 1367. And now we come to Coney Street, the name dating from the time of the Anglo-Saxon occupation, from the word 'Cyning', meaning king. Turn left here and the road leads to St Mary's Abbey, where a devout Benedictine order observed its worship. Turn right and it's the castle, looking down over the city from its high motte. Peace and devotion one way, war and bloodshed the other; almost a metaphor for the city itself.

But continue on, and now we're in Pavement, where proclamations are heard and traitors lose their heads. Here is the hustle and bustle of the market, where hardworking farmers and merchants try to earn an honest crust from the fruits of their labours, while cutpurses and vagabonds try to relieve them of the same. On the left here is the Shambles, the dingy street of butchers' shops, where the rich warm smells of blood and freshly cut muscle and sinew mingle with the sweat of the brows of porters and slaughtermen. And that leads us to Petergate, a street whose most famous son dreamed of regicide, and earned an ignominious traitor's death and an infamy, the legacy of which continues to this day.

And finally, emerging from this street we find ourselves at Windy Corner, here in the shadow of the towers of the minster church, where local legend says that the wind and the devil came to cause mischief: Satan made the wind promise to wait for him outside while he went in to cause terror, but never returned, so the wind is still there.

This huge cathedral, the largest such Gothic structure in Northern Europe, towers over the town, dominating the skyline with its 200ft central tower, its huge imposing walls and vast swathes of medieval stained glass. It stands on a spot where a church has stood to the glory of God since the first humble wooden building, erected by St Paulinus in AD 627, and before that the Great Hall of the Roman camp, where five emperors broke bread with the soldiers of their empire. Demolished and rebuilt, damaged by weather and wind and burned to the ground several times, the current structure dates back to 1220, and within its walls have walked kings and commoners, heroes and villains, saints and sinners. Through it all, it has remained the beating heart of the city.

So take a walk through this city, through this capital of the North. Marvel at its riches and its splendours; meet the people, learn their names; you'll get a hearty Yorkshire welcome here. Just don't go too far into those dark corners, or you maybe surprised by what you discover lurking there.

Alan Sharp, 2015

JANUARY

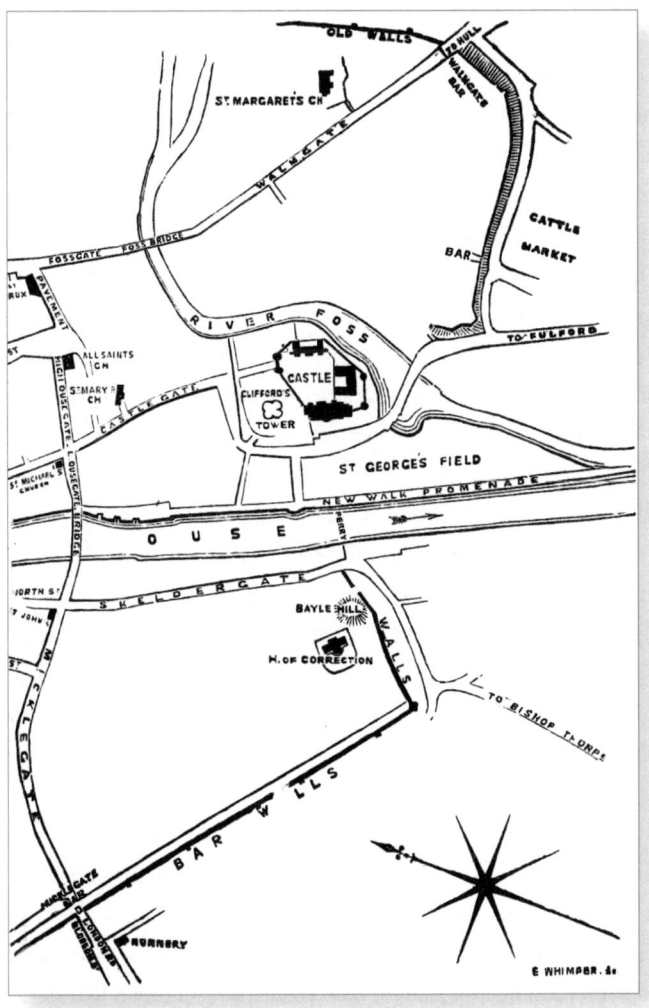

Map showing the location and layout of York Castle and other important surrounding buildings in the eighteenth century. (Author's collection)

1 JANUARY 1660 The Siege of York and subsequent Battle of Marston Moor, both described elsewhere in this book, were the turning point in the English Civil War which resulted in Charles I having his head removed. This date saw York play an equally vital role in its restoration, and the same man, Thomas Fairfax, was the architect of both sets of events. After Oliver Cromwell's death, and the resignation of his son Richard from the role of Lord Protector, Fairfax became convinced that no Member of Parliament was fit to lead, and that the monarchy must return. He was joined in this belief by General Monck, the Governor of Scotland, and after a daring ten-day ride by Fairfax's cousin Brian to communicate between the two men, Fairfax promised to take the field and secure York on this date. On the day, Fairfax was ill with gout, but nothing would stop him fulfilling his promise. The country was by now under the control of the Committee of Safety, and their leading general, John Lambert, was advancing north with an army of 10,000 men. However, one of his officers, Colonel Redman, indicated that he was willing to side with Fairfax, and the two armies met at the historic battlefield at Marston Moor where sixteen years earlier, Fairfax and Cromwell had slaughtered the armies of York. As Fairfax arrived, Lambert's army approached him with a paper stating that they stood with Parliament, and in full view of Lambert's troops, with only a ragtag army of local nobles behind him, Fairfax tore the paper to pieces. No sooner had he done so than regiment after regiment of Lambert's army began to leave his ranks and move over to Fairfax's side. With his new army, Fairfax left the battlefield and rode into York to secure it for Monck's arrival.

2 JANUARY 1835 A group of men were at work on some restoration work high up in the prayer house of York Minster when a section of the scaffolding on which they were standing gave way. There were five men on the section at the time, and they were all plunged to the ground, sustaining severe injuries. The height at which they were working was said to be approximately 30–40ft. The foreman of the works, a Mr Scott, was killed instantly in the fall, while the other four were conducted to York County Hospital for treatment.

3 JANUARY 1885 Magistrates in York spent the entire day untangling a web of different assault cases all tied to the same incident. From the various details, it appears that it all started when a boy named John Willis was bitten by a dog owned by Thomas Mercer of Lowther Street. On the day in question, Mercer had heard a knock at the door, and on opening it, a gang of men rushed in and began to attack all inside. James Gowthorpe dragged Mercer outside and beat him with a stick, while his wife Martha was struck in the face by Thomas Willis, the boy's father, resulting in a broken nose

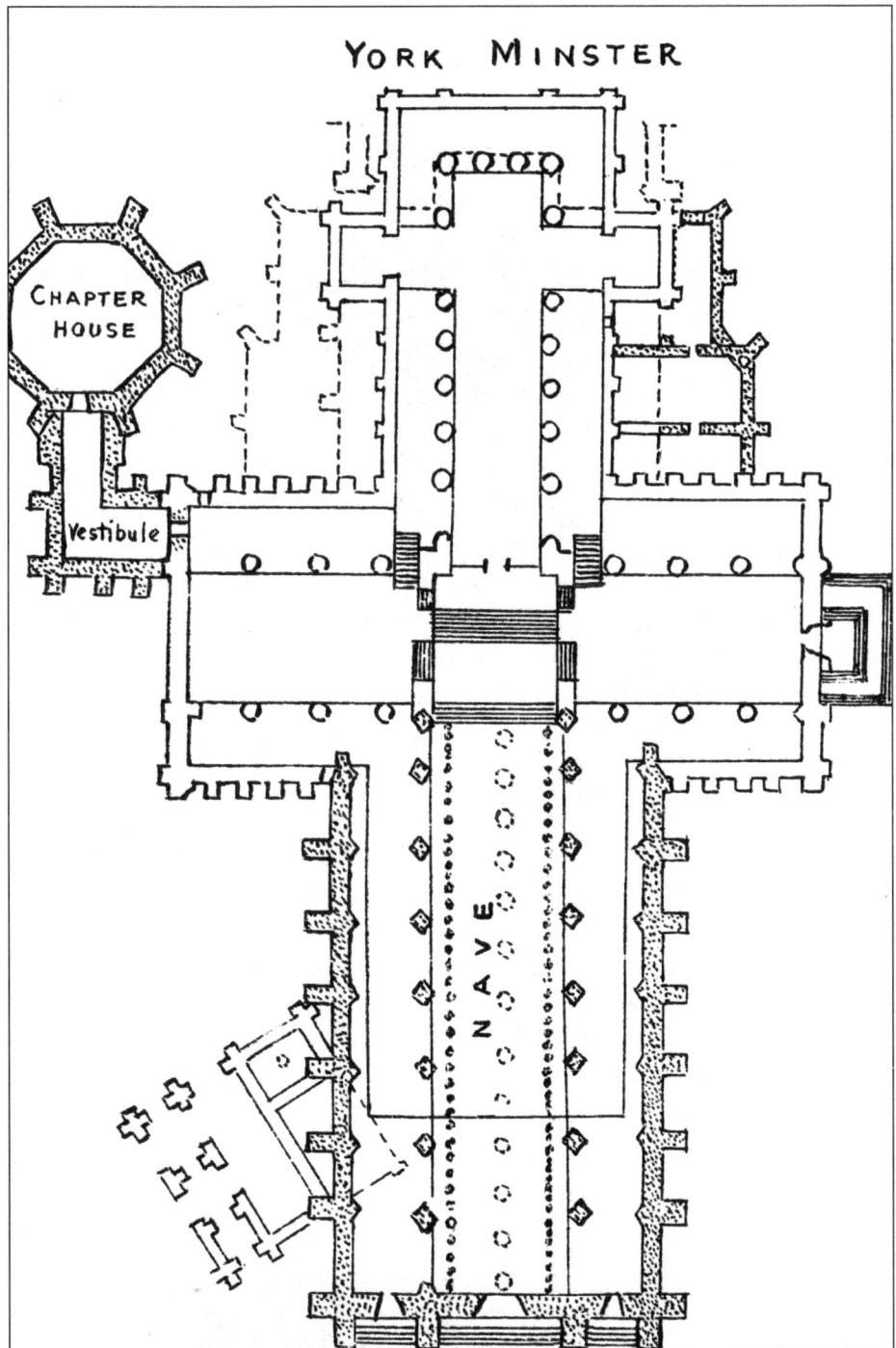

Nineteenth-century floor plan of York Minster. (Author's collection)

and bleeding from her mouth. Willis then chased Mercer's daughter Mary Ann into the kitchen, where she defended herself with a fire poker. During this she saw through the window of the kitchen that four other men were beating her brother Henry in the yard, although she could not identify them. She then ran to the bedroom, chased by three men, who were about to assault her when the police arrived. The men then set about the two policemen, one of whom, PC Paul, was severely injured in a brutal attack during which he was kicked and beaten into unconsciousness. Gowthorpe, Willis and another man named John Haigh were all sentenced to lengthy terms of imprisonment.

4 JANUARY 1786 Some stories you really want to know more details about. The parish register of the church of St Mary in Castlegate records the death on this date of a gentleman named George Birch. The details of his death read 'most improperly laid before the fire when half frozen'. He was buried in the churchyard four days later.

5 JANUARY 1649 Isabella Billington has become one of the best known Yorkshire witches, although in truth very little is known about her. Most likely her infamy stems from the severity of her crime. She was from Pocklington, around 12 miles east of the city, and the records state that on this date she crucified her mother, before offering a calf and a cockerel as a burnt sacrifice to the Devil. Why she did this was never made apparent. Isabella was tried at York Castle and found guilty of witchcraft; she was sentenced to first be hanged, and then her body burned at the stake. Her husband was also sentenced to death for being complicit in the crime.

6 JANUARY 1565 Until the 1840s, the Ouse Bridge was the only crossing over the river other than by ferry boat. A bridge was first built on the current site during the days of the Viking settlement, that one being a wooden construction, around 270 yards along the river from the site of the original Roman bridge. By the mid-sixteenth century, an impressive bridge stood in the location, topped with shops and other buildings along its entire length. It was supported by St William's chapel at one end, and included a prison in its structure, as well as the first public lavatory in the city, constructed in 1367. However, in 1564, Yorkshire endured a hard winter with heavy rainfall, and the River Ouse became swollen. As the winter grew colder, water started to freeze around the pillars of the bridge. Then, on this date, a sudden thaw occurred, and water began to flow around the pillars, which had been damaged by the ice, causing them to collapse. The bridge fell into the river, twelve of its buildings collapsing with it and dropping many of the people into the icy cold waters. Some managed to scramble to the banks, but twelve in total were killed and many others suffered permanent injury through frostbite.

The Ouse Bridge, around 1800, painted by Thomas Girtin. Repaired after being partially damaged in 1565, it was dismantled to build the current bridge in 1810. (Author's collection)

7 JANUARY 1896 Henry Lund, a platelayer working on the York to Malton railway line near Flaxton, was knocked down by a train and killed despite nothing untoward appearing to have happened. Those who were with him stated that the morning was dark and misty, but both he and the train, which was shunting and hence moving slowly, were carrying lights and so each should have been aware of the presence of the other. Those involved in shunting the train asserted that it was done in the usual way, and that at no point were the crew aware of the presence of anyone on the line. Lund himself said nothing, in fact when he was found he was said to have groaned twice and then expired.

8 JANUARY 1813 Between 1811 and 1813, Yorkshire was a frequent venue for Luddite activity. The Luddite movement was protesting against the industrialisation of the textile industry, meaning that unskilled labour could cheaply be employed to do the work previously carried out by highly skilled workers. Mill owners regularly had to protect their property from attack, and one such, William Horsfall, had stated that he would 'ride up to his saddle in Luddite blood'. As a result, George Mellor, William Thorpe and Thomas Smith lay in wait to ambush him one night, and in the ensuing fight Mellor shot Horsfall in the groin, causing him to bleed to death. The three men were arrested and hanged on this date at York Castle. Two troops of cavalry had to be positioned around the entrances to the castle to prevent any attempt to rescue them. A week later, a total of fourteen men were hanged on the same day for Luddite activities including riot and acts of theft of arms or money.

9 JANUARY 780 Eighth-century politics in the Kingdom of Northumbria were a violent and bloody process by which kings and nobles were regularly deposed in battle or by murder. When Aethelred I, who had come to the throne at the age of 12, was deposed five years later in 779, following the assassination – probably on his orders – of three of his ealdormen (or earls), his closest advisor, Osbald, worked hard to restore him. Aelfwald became king, but on this date Osbald and another man named Athelheard gathered a force intending to end Aelfwald's reign. In a place called Seletune, said to be north of York and probably corresponding to the modern village of Silton, they approached a house where Aelfwald regularly stayed and burned it to the ground. Aelfwald was not present, but his son Bearn was inside and died in the flames. This attempted coup was unsuccessful and Aelfwald reigned for a further nine years before his own death. In 790, Aethelred returned to the throne and restored Osbald to his previous position. On Aethelred's death Osbald himself was crowned king, but reigned for only twenty-seven days before abdicating and exiling himself at Lindesfarne. On his death, his body was returned to York and buried in the minster.

10 JANUARY 1675 Mr George Aisleby was married to the second daughter of Sir John Mallory, whose older sister was staying as a guest with the family. One night in early January, they all attended a ball at the York apartments of the Duke of Buckingham, and Aisleby and his wife left early, trusting a servant to return home with the sister. However, a friend of Aisleby's, one Jonathon Jennings, discovered the sister, who was

Goodramgate and the Monk Bar, photographed in the 1930s. (Author's collection)

unaware of the arrangement. He put her in his carriage and tried to return her to Aisleby's home, but found the place locked up and no answer at the door. He therefore took the girl back to his own lodgings to stay the night. Aisleby was convinced some impropriety had taken place and sent a servant on this morning to Jennings with a letter stating that they should meet to discuss matters relating to the honour of the Mallory family. Aisleby is said to have awaited Jennings' arrival outside the Monk Bar, and the two then went to Penley Crofts, a short distance outside the city walls. There, Aisleby drew his sword and charged at Jennings who, after backing off as far as he could, drew his own weapon to defend himself. During the fight, Jennings was wounded in the hand, but Aisleby received a severe laceration to his right arm from which he later bled to death. Jennings was initially charged and found guilty of manslaughter, but received a royal pardon.

11 **JANUARY 1655** Henry Hatefield made a deposition at York Castle that one Katherine Earle had struck him on the neck with the stalk of a dock plant and then did the same to his horse, which immediately fell sick and died, while he himself also felt ill. He stated that she had previously clapped a Mr Frank, of his acquaintance, on the back, and that Mr Frank had then also felt sick and had gone home and died shortly afterwards, complaining throughout his illness that Earle had bewitched him. Earle was taken into custody and, upon examination two marks were found on her body, which were taken to be the signs of a witch. She is said to have complained that one of the marks came as a result of a burn. There is no record of what happened to her but, historically, such evidence against her suggests that she would have been put to death.

12 **JANUARY 1913** Eliza Halder lived with her husband in Lower Eldon Street, where he kept a scrap dealership in a warehouse at the back. She had been ill and confined to bed, and while he was working, their servant had brought some breakfast and lit a fire in the bedroom. A short while afterwards the servant heard a commotion and Mrs Halder came running down the stairs, her clothes ablaze. A neighbour, Morris Cooke, was alerted by his wife that something was wrong in the Halder house and ran across the road. Entering the house, he saw Mrs Halder screaming and in flames, and quickly picked up a nearby hearthrug and threw it over her, laying her down and smothering the flames. Meanwhile, Mr Halder had heard the shouts and come back from his warehouse. Mrs Halder was promptly conveyed to the hospital, and on the way she told her husband that she had sat too close to the fire and set alight her bedsock, which had then ignited the rest of her clothing. Her burns were too severe for any hope of recovery and she died at around 3 p.m.

13 JANUARY 1686 During the reign of King James II, large religious services became fraught with danger, as the populace feared that the openly Catholic king was going to restore the nation to Catholicism. On this date, Lady Henrietta Stanley, wife of the Earl of Strafford, was to be buried in great ceremony in York Minster. To ensure that the funeral went smoothly, Sir John Reresby ordered his company of grenadiers to accompany the hearse. Around forty soldiers lined up on either side as the coffin was paraded through the Micklegate Bar and brought through the streets to the minster, but the presence of the military seems to have antagonised the crowds rather than subduing them, and a riot ensued. The soldiers were set upon with sticks and rocks thrown by the mob, while the metal fittings were torn from the coffin and the black cloth that lay over it was stolen. The soldiers managed to get the coffin into the minster, and found that they had to stand guard at the door of the choir while the rioters tried to force their way in. Eventually the company retired from the church to the Minster Yard, hoping that in a less enclosed space they could control the riot, but they continued to be bombarded with everything the mob could lay their hands on. Several of the soldiers were seriously injured, including one Sergeant Fowler, who was said to be in danger of losing his eyes. Finally the company broke and fled through the city streets in disarray, still chased by angry citizens.

14 JANUARY 1809 Jonathan Graham was a young man of respectable family who became enamoured with the daughter of a farmer named William Jeft, who kept a farm near York. Graham courted and married the girl, and they began to reside in her father's house, where he took on the role of farm manager. However, his ambitions extended further, and on this date he went to a neighbour, George Hartley, and asked to borrow a gun. Hartley was unable to help him at that time, but he requested again several times and eventually Hartley obliged. Graham then arranged for his wife and child to visit his brother-in-law and, after they were gone, told his wife's mother that he would follow. A few hours after leaving the house, a gunshot was heard, and Jeft was later found with a serious gunshot injury which was considered life threatening but from which he eventually recovered. In a magnificent display of stupidity, when apprehended, Graham stated that the police could not charge him with the crime because 'nobody saw me shoot him'. He was sentenced to death and executed at York a few weeks later.

15 JANUARY 1916 Private William Laws, of the 2/7th Northumberland Fusilliers, was stationed in York and billeted at the Fishergate Council School, and had been given leave to visit his family in Newcastle. He returned to York apparently in good

health, but on this date began to complain of stomach pains, which became worse as the day went on. At around midnight he was disturbing the whole building – running around and screaming that he was going to die – to the extent that he was locked in the guard room, but on his quietening down it was seen that he had slumped against the wall semi-conscious, and so a doctor was called. However, before the medical man could arrive, Laws had expired. It transpired that during his time in Newcastle, he had been taking medicine for some malady, but had accidentally picked up rat poison and taken that instead, and this had slowly eaten away at the lining of his stomach, causing it to rupture.

16 JANUARY 1883 Private John Maher, of the 5th Dragoon Guards stationed in the city, was given a pass of leave until midnight of this night, and was seen by a PC Taylor heading across the city from the direction of Hungate. As Taylor watched, Maher climbed over a wall and began to walk down the bank of the river, which was flooded over its banks at the time, making the edge difficult to see. At some point the policeman noticed that the soldier had disappeared from sight, even though he should not have gone so far in the time, and he realised that the man had walked straight off the riverbank and into the river. Being on the other bank, he was unable to lend any assistance, and so rushed to the nearest bridge and crossed over but when he reached the spot, the other man was nowhere to be found. His body was discovered floating in the river at 7 a.m. the following day by a lamplighter doing his rounds.

17 JANUARY 1729 An article in the *York Courant* tells us that on this date 'a sad accident happened here, viz., a boy about 12 years old belonging to a vessel at the staith, having business to go to the top mast, was of a sudden blown therefrom by the great wind at that time, into the river, and drowned. He is not as yet found.'

18 JANUARY 1896 The *Yorkshire Gazette* reported on the death of a Mr Kirk, of Bishop Monckton, who had been killed while riding in a hunt with the York and Ainsty hounds. The gentleman had been riding in the hunt since a youth, and now, at 76 years of age, he was said to have been hunting for sixty years. Despite this, Kirk was still a hard rider. However, while attempting to jump a hedge to follow the hounds, his horse struck a cross bar with its forelegs and turned over entirely, landing on top of the unfortunate man. By the time the other riders reached him, it was found that his neck was broken and he must have died almost instantly.

19 JANUARY 1884 A report in the *York Herald* on this date tells the story that some nights earlier John Lamb, gamekeeper for a Mr Bateson-de-Yarborough, was watching on that gentleman's lands when he heard a gunshot. He called on his assistant, James Salmon, and the two began to search the land thereabouts when they heard a second shot. Salmon then spotted a man running from a hedgerow, and the pair took off in pursuit. As they crossed an open field, the man turned and pointed a shotgun at them, then, thinking better of it, held the gun by the barrel and threatened to strike them with it. The two men overpowered him and on inspection found that the gun was indeed loaded. The culprit turned out to be a labourer named Joseph Andrews, who had twenty-one previous convictions. On being led from the court having been sentenced to six months' hard labour, he shouted, 'I'll have a few more when I have done!'

20 JANUARY 1891 The winter of 1890 is remembered as one of the coldest in York's history. A continuous fifty-eight-day cold snap began on 25 November of the previous year; during this period average snowfall was between 8 and 10 inches per day, and temperatures regularly dropped below -10°C. The poorer citizens were at grave risk of starvation or freezing to death, so an emergency meeting had to be held by the Lord Mayor of the city to discuss relief for those in need and an emergency committee to take control of the situation was appointed to begin operations on this date. On its first morning alone, it is reported that 3,233 quarts of soup were distributed by soup kitchens around the city. The cold snap ended just a few days later, but the thaw that followed caused widespread flooding, so things scarcely improved for the next month.

21 JANUARY 1804 Hartley Hemmet, convicted of stealing a box containing wearing apparel, the property of Margaret Dickinson, was sentenced by the quarter sessions of the court at York, to be kept at hard labour for three months, and to be publicly whipped through the streets of the city from the House of Corrections to the Pavement Cross on this date.

22 JANUARY 1875 A report in the *York Herald* tells of a woman named Barnes and her nephew, who lived in a house on Heworth Moor, and are described as being 'peculiar and of weak intellect'. The local youth had apparently begun to victimise the pair, and regularly threw stones at their house, breaking the windows, to the point where they had been forced to board up the windows and barricade themselves in. A few days earlier, two policemen named Dean and Steel had called at the house to check that the pair were in good health when a group of about twenty boys

assembled outside and started to attack the property. When the policemen emerged, most of them ran away but a few were apprehended. Mr Alderman March, who had befriended the pair, spoke on their behalf in court, saying that some severe action needed to be taken to stop this happening again. The Lord Mayor ordered each of the boys fined 20s, which would have been nearly a week's wages for the average family at this time.

23 JANUARY 1671 A scuffle in the street almost escalated into something much more serious. Two men were engaging in a dogfight in Micklegate, their animals making a dreadful noise, when a soldier named Hodgson came out of a nearby house and ordered them to desist. When they failed to do so, Hodgson drew his sword and sliced open the cheek of one of the men. One of the sheriff's men by the name of Perott was nearby and ordered Hodgson to put up his sword, whereupon Hodgson told him he would not, and that he would run the official through if he tried to force him. Perott then left to bring back other officials to arrest the man, and as he was leaving, Hodgson shouted after him that he was a 'pale-faced rascal'. Hodgson was arrested, taken before the Lord Mayor the following day and bound over to keep the peace.

24 JANUARY 1912 Kate Bennett, a schoolteacher, was returning to her home in Richardson Street at around midday on this date when she heard the sound of someone in distress in the home of her neighbours, William and Henrietta Hodgson. Running inside, she found Mrs Hodgson lying in front of the fire, engulfed in flames. Taking up a rug and quickly stifling the fire, she found that the unfortunate woman had burns across most of her body and her hair was completely burned off. Doctors were called and she was rushed to York County Hospital, but her injuries were too extensive and she died later that day. Mrs Bennett was at a loss as to what had caused the accident as she recalled that there was only a small fire in the fireplace, and it did not seem as if Mrs Hodgson had been cooking on it or tending to it.

25 JANUARY 1663 Following the Restoration of the Monarchy in 1660, a number of disenfranchised Parliamentarian groups attempted to reverse this situation. In 1662, one group in Yorkshire called for a 'righteous and glorious strife', and for people to rise up, come forward and join a noble band of staunch patriots to defend their rights against injustice and oppression. A date was arranged for those answering the call to appear in arms in Farnley Wood, near Otley. However, the date and time having been widely distributed, the authorities were aware of what was due to happen

and a large body of regular troops and militia awaited their arrival. A commission was set up in York to try the leaders of the uprising, and eighteen of them, mostly conventional preachers and former Parliamentarian soldiers, were sentenced to be executed on this date at the Knavesmire. Following the executions, their heads were removed and set up on the various city gates, and two of the men were quartered and their body parts displayed in a similar fashion.

26 JANUARY 1777 Press gangs were a hated part of life in England in the eighteenth century. Arriving in town to recruit volunteers for the naval forces, they were empowered to sign up anyone between the ages of 18 and 55 who they had reason to believe had seafaring experience. Often, though, they would use a very loose application of these regulations, and many pressed into service could find themselves signed up for many years. Having allowed a press gang to operate in the city, on this morning the Lord Mayor of York received the following letter: 'My Lord, you may take this for a warning, that if you do not send the press gang out of York before next Tuesday, you may expect your own house set on fire, and the Mansion House too. There is 273 young men set their hands to a paper to put the above into execution.'

27 JANUARY 1929 A young private in the Royal North Lancashire Regiment was being transported to York Barracks, where he was to serve a period of detention in a military prison for desertion. On the journey he requested permission to use the lavatory, but once inside he broke a window and climbed out on to the roof of the train. Once his absence was noticed, his escort pulled the communication cord, bringing the train to a sudden stop and throwing the young man from the top. Injured and bleeding, he crawled underneath the train and was captured soon afterwards, making a run for a nearby quarry.

28 JANUARY 1884 William Wyld was a 72-year-old former York rugby league player who still had connections to the club and was said to keep himself in good condition. He was found stabbed to death in his home in Huntingdon Road, having put up such a fierce struggle that the muscles of his arms were said to have burst from the strain. He had visited the rugby league ground the day before, and at the time he had mentioned withdrawing £800; he was a man known to keep money around his house and to lend it out liberally. After his death, £72 was found hidden in a box in his gas cooker. The police investigation took several weeks but eventually a man named John Dand was arrested. A native of Kirkcaldy in Scotland, Dand was

working in York and was known to have spent time with Wyld. On his arrest he is said to have told police that the two had argued about money and that he had killed him by accident, although he later retracted this and claimed he was not at the house when Wyld died. However, evidence of Wyld's blood on his clothes was enough to convince a jury and he was sentenced to death and hanged in Manchester on 12 June.

29 JANUARY 1803 The *York Herald* of this date reported on a group of highwaymen who robbed a post boy on the road from York to Northallerton. The trio consisted of two men on horseback and one on foot, and they got away with a sum of £1 2s. However, the pedestrian of the three, whose name was Gamble, was later arrested trying to steal a saddle, and confessed to all. He also stated that the boy had not been their intended target, the group having set out to rob the mailcoach travelling north – a much more lucrative affair – but they had been delayed by other carts on the road. The coach driver had spotted them and blew his horn to scare their horses as they approached.

30 JANUARY 1747 Travelling to York from the village of Shipton, about 5 miles north, William Houseman was robbed in a lane by two highwaymen who got away with a purse containing some silver and other coins. The amount of money was minimal, but to Houseman it was the principle involved, and so he quickly rode into Shipton, rounded up three other men and all four armed themselves before heading out on the common again. On arriving at the spot, the same two men were laying in wait and Houseman called out to them, whereupon they advanced on him. As they approached, he fired his pistol and wounded one of the men in the thigh. They both attempted to fire back but one missed and the other one's gun failed to go off. The men then turned and fled, but Houseman and his party set off in pursuit. Houseman managed to catch up to one, named Edward Equall, and struck him with the butt of his pistol several times, finally succeeding in taking him prisoner, but the other man managed to escape. Another man named Shepard later came forward and stated that he had been robbed by the same two men in the same spot an hour earlier that evening.

31 JANUARY 1891 In a rather bizarre incident, 50-year-old William Melville walked into a police station in Gateshead on this night in a drunken state, telling police that he wanted to confess to a murder. However, he was too inebriated at the time to make any sense, so it wasn't until Monday (two days later) that he made a

statement to the effect that twenty-five years earlier, he and another man named William Jobling had taken a train to York, where they intended to break into houses. Having found a likely one, they got inside and managed to find £27 in money, but as they departed down a back staircase they were stopped by a girl who tried to raise an alarm. As a result, Melville had raised a revolver and shot her dead. He and the other man then rushed to the railway station and escaped to Manchester. This information was communicated to the York police, who made a thorough search of their records and could find no instance of such an event ever taking place.

FEBRUARY

The Devil in York – this sixteenth-century carving was actually the sign of a printer's shop in Stonegate. (Author's collection)

1 FEBRUARY 1829 Jonathan Martin lived a varied life. As a sailor in the Royal Navy, he served at the Battle of Copenhagen, where his shipmates spoke of his religious obsession. He later became a Wesleyan minister, but his odd, obsessive behaviour, which included threatening to shoot the Bishop of Oxford, resulted in him being made unwelcome within that Church. Eventually he ended up in York, where he objected to members of the clergy at the minster moving in high social circles, and constantly left threatening notes pinned up around the area. One night, while asleep, he dreamed of a dark cloud that moved over the minster, and became convinced that God had instructed him to burn the place down. On this date he hid out in the choir of the minster until everyone had gone. Then he set fire to the woodwork and escaped through a window. The fire was not spotted until 7 a.m. the next day, by which time it was out of control and remained so until it burned through the timbers of the roof, which collapsed, smothering much of the flames. Even so, it took a further two days to extinguish it completely. At the height of the fire, hot air is said to have been forced through the organ pipes, causing a haunting discordant cacophony as firefighters attempted to bring the blaze under control. Martin was tried for arson but escaped the death penalty due to his mental instability, and was instead confined to the Bedlam asylum for the rest of his life.

2 FEBRUARY 1904 Walking beside the River Ouse on this morning, William Lund saw a woman with a baby in her arms letting herself through the gate near the Scarborough railway bridge and set off along the path in the direction of Lendal Bridge. Without warning, she ran down the bank and threw herself into the river, at

The Scarborough Railway Bridge across the River Ouse. (Author's collection)

which point she began to be swept away by the water. Disregarding his own safety, Lund plunged into the river himself and succeeded in reaching the woman and keeping her afloat while another man on the bank, John Ankers, located a lifebuoy and threw it to him. By now others had arrived and together they succeeded in taking both woman and child out of the water. The woman's name was Georgina Pitts, and she had recently separated from her husband, a railwayman, on the grounds that he kept her without money or food and she had had to pawn almost all her belongings as a result. She had been staying with her sister, but knew that she was a drain on the other woman's resources and could not stand to be the cause of financial distress.

3 FEBRUARY 1816 George Lofthouse, a wheelwright from Leeds, had some business in York on this date and so caught the mailcoach to travel to the city. Along the way the coach stopped at a public house where Lofthouse alighted and went for a drink. Unfortunately, while he was inside refreshing himself, some scuffle or fracas began to occur outside and the coach driver, not wanting to be caught up in it, drove away. Seeing the coach depart, Lofthouse began to run after it, and chased the coach for around a mile before collapsing at the side of the road in an exhausted state. Such an exhausted state, in fact, that he never recovered and died the following morning.

4 FEBRUARY 211 This date marks the death of Septimius Severus, the Roman emperor who ruled for the last few years of his life from Eboracum, the fort standing on the land that is now York. Severus is remembered as the first African to hold the position of emperor, having been born in the area of modern-day Libya. A leading general in the Roman Army before his ascent to leadership, Severus was a warlike emperor who came to Britain to subdue the tribes of Caledonia and, in doing so, instructed his army to 'let no one escape sheer destruction ... not even the babe in the womb of the mother, if it be male'. He had seized power for himself with the support of his army after the assassination of two previous emperors, Commodus and Pertinax. He died in the city after a short illness, which some ascribe to gout, but rumours have persisted that he was in fact poisoned by his son, Caracalla, who succeeded him.

Bust of Septimius Severus. (Author's collection)

5 FEBRUARY 1875 An inquest was held in York into the discovery, a few days earlier, of the body of a newborn male infant in Cinder Lane, off Marygate. On discovery, it was said to have been evident that death had been brought about deliberately because the head was severely swollen. Medical evidence showed that death had been the result of a fracture of the skull and an effusion of blood to the brain, which would have been caused by a blow to the head. A verdict of 'wilful murder against some person or persons unknown' was returned. The case was never solved.

6 FEBRUARY 1842 At around 11.45 p.m., Mrs Sarah Sunderland of Lawrence Street was summoned by her neighbour, George Stokes, to attend to his wife who, he told her, was in a bad way. When she arrived at the couple's bedroom, she found the woman to be dead. Mrs Stokes was in her early thirties and had delivered a child six months earlier, but the family were in straitened circumstances and what money they could get was spent on a little meagre food, barely enough to live on. The deceased having had a tapeworm until some months before, a doctor had given her some medicine to quit herself of it but this had only exacerbated this situation. A few days before her death, she had been talking to another neighbour, Mary Burton, about the fact that her arms had grown so thin that you could see the bones. Doctors examining her body confirmed that the woman had indeed died of starvation.

7 FEBRUARY 1922 Walter Ford had suffered a spinal injury at his place of work in a Tyneside shipyard some years before, and had since been out of work. Having formed an attachment to Lucy Newton, against the wishes of her parents, the couple had decided to elope, and boarded a train at Sunderland, bound for Bristol. Not wishing to arouse suspicion, they initially travelled in separate compartments, but later moved to the same one. As the train approached York, Ms Newton got up to fix a problem with the window and, as she did, she felt a stinging sensation in her side. She turned, shocked, and saw Ford holding a gun to his own head, which he then fired. Ms Newton alerted those in the next compartment and the conductor arrived. He found Ford to be dead from his head wound and that Ms Newton had been shot in her side. An entry in Ford's diary suggested that the pair had agreed on a suicide pact, but the girl claimed that he had never spoken to her about anything of that nature.

8 FEBRUARY 1910 A group of signal fitters from the Leeman Road depot in York were out on the Leeds to Normanton railway track at Askham Bog, on the outskirts of the city, when one of the men, Thomas Shepherdson, needed to get something from

the signal box on the other side of the track. Unfortunately, he seems to have failed to notice the approach of the Great Central Railway express train, which struck him full on and at high speed. Unsurprisingly, he was killed instantly.

9 FEBRUARY 1898 Mary Carter, of Portland Place in Layerthorpe, was prone to epileptic fits, which had made it difficult for her to find work, so she stayed at home and kept house for her father. On this date, when he returned home from work, he found the 17 year old lying in his fireplace, burned to death. It was surmised by the doctors that she had suffered a fit and fallen into the fire, where her clothes would have quickly ignited and caused burns all across her body too that were severe to survive.

10 FEBRUARY 1876 Charles Coates, of Lowther Street, was committed to one month's hard labour on this date for assaulting his wife. He was described as a violent man, who had mistreated her on many occasions before, resulting in a number of spells of hospitalisation. On this occasion, he is said to have flown into a rage after she asked him for a shilling to pay a debt. Coates struck her, and when she fell to the ground, began repeatedly kicking at her body and face.

11 FEBRUARY 1883 The pain of a urinary infection has been said to be so extreme as to drive people insane. Such was the case with John Cresser of White Horse Passage, who came to the end of his tether. He had suffered from the ailment for several years, and had recently undergone an operation that was supposed to have cured him, and which for a short while appeared to have done so. However, when the condition began to reimpose itself, Cresser could take no more, took up a razor and slit his throat so violently that the coroner stated he would likely have died almost instantly.

12 FEBRUARY 1895 After several days during which the mean temperature had not risen above freezing, the River Ouse was frozen over, and by Sunday, 10 February, the popular pastime of skating was being enjoyed on its surface. The authorities were quick to put out warning signs on those parts of the river where the ice was

not considered sufficient to hold a person's weight; however, two separate incidents on the river resulted in death. In the first, three students at the Diocesan Training College skated too close to the sewage pumping station at Fulford: one, John Raine, fell through the ice and was drowned. In the second, one of the masters of St Peter's School was skating into the city from Popplewell with a companion when they came across two men who had fallen through and were clinging to the edge of the ice. They managed to pull the men to safety, but it transpired that a third, Edward Murray of Heworth, had sunk beneath the water and disappeared from their sight.

13 FEBRUARY 1750 After many weeks of almost incessant rain storms, the *York Courant* reported that 'the north post, due yesterday morning about eleven, did not come in till nine at night. The River Ouse is swelled higher than ever was known in the memory of man. And yesterday one John Saville, coming with the post-chaise from Easingwold, was drowned near the Blue Bridge in Skelton Lane, about two miles from this city. As the waters are so excessively out in all parts of the country, it is hoped our customers will excuse us if they are not served so early as usual.'

14 FEBRUARY 1789 On this date, Robert Wilkinson was executed for a highway robbery committed in Dunnington, a parish on the outskirts of York. Wilkinson netted 1 guinea 9*s* and a silver watch during the robbery in question and he is said to have 'used his victim in a cruel manner'. He was convicted after his partner in the robbery turned King's Evidence. In a letter written to his wife he describes a meeting with his father: 'Just after I had received my sentence, my aged father followed me to the Castle, dejected and sorrowful, almost terrifying me as much as my sentence, when he wrung my hand and burst into a flood of tears crying, "oh, my son, my most unfortunate son! After all my care and diligence bestowed upon you, have I reared you up for the gallow tree?"'

15 FEBRUARY 1893 An inquest into the death of William Scott of no fixed abode provided an example of no good deed going unpunished. Scott had worked as a farmhand for a man named Taylor, whose farm was at Askham Bryan. Having turned up at the farm earlier in the week claiming to be destitute, Scott asked if he might find some food and somewhere to sleep. Taylor, taking pity, provided him with a good meal and allowed him to bed down in one of his cowsheds. The following morning, when another farmhand had entered the cowshed, he found it filled with smoke. The straw on which Scott had slept had burned up and his body was a blackened husk within it. A clay pipe close to the body suggested he had lit this and then fallen asleep, failing to wake when the straw caught on fire. The cowshed contained Taylor's five best cows, worth a considerable amount of money, and all were found dead, asphyxiated by the smoke of the fire.

16 FEBRUARY 1828 The murder of John Dyon, shot dead as he entered the gate of his home near Doncaster on this date, led to the trial, conviction and execution at York Castle of the man's brother, William, and William's son, also called John, in a case which gripped the nation. The motive, it was claimed, was due to the father of the brothers favouring John's family in terms of inheritance over William's. The pair came under suspicion because they had been seen at the house of the deceased a week before carrying guns – which they claimed were for hunting, even though there was no hunting at that time of year – and enquiring what time the man generally returned from market. They were arrested but released on having a strong alibi that they were at home eating supper at the time of the murder. However, William's son-in-law and servant, who had provided this alibi, both later confessed to having given false evidence, and that the men did not return home until after midnight that night. Other evidence that suggested their innocence was that the impressions of boots in the snow at the crime scene were the wrong size, but boots were later found in their possession which did exactly match, and lastly that two men seen loitering nearby did not match their description, but it was eventually decided that these men had no part in the crime.

17 FEBRUARY 1883 Joseph Binns was a farm labourer in the employment of James Craven of Fulford. On this night Binns, along with another farmhand known only as Jack, was seen on the road headed towards Craven's property coming from the Barrack Tavern somewhat the worse for drink. A witness them stated that Binns had threatened to kill Jack before striking him and, at around midnight that night, Jack was found lying at the side of the road in a desperate condition, dying shortly afterwards without speaking a word. The next morning, Binns told his fellow workers that he and Jack had been attacked by two men, and that he had left Jack lying by the road because he couldn't get him home. He later retracted this statement, and claimed that he had been trying to get Jack home when the two men had fallen and he had skinned his nose and face and so decided to leave Jack there. The medical evidence showed that Jack had died of exposure, and at the inquest a verdict of death by misadventure was recorded, with the coroner stating that Binns, while not legally obliged to carry his co-worker home, deserved the severest censure for not having done so.

18 FEBRUARY 1875 Henry Cooper, a man living in Barker Hill, was walking down Thief Lane on this date when he spotted something lying in a ditch near to the railway works, which on closer inspection turned out to be the naked body of a child. He went immediately to the York police office and reported the discovery, and the child was found to be a female, probably between 15 and 18 months old. There were no marks of violence, and the child did not appear to be malnourished in any way so it was decided that she had probably died of natural causes and that the family had been unable to afford the funeral expenses. At first the lack of clothes was thought to be due to neglect, but later another man was arrested after selling the clothes of a child of about that age, which he claimed to have found in the vicinity.

19 FEBRUARY 1408 The Battle of Bramham Moor, which took place a small distance west of York, was the final battle of the Percy Uprising. This had begun six years earlier when King Henry IV, whom the Percy family had supported during his coup against his cousin Richard II, had demanded that Henry Percy, 1st Earl of Northumberland, hand over all prisoners from the Battle of Homildon Hill in return for a small amount of compensation. Under normal circumstances Percy would have been able to ransom the nobles in his possession for his own profit, and was naturally upset that the king was attempting to usurp this. As a result, he allied his family to Edmund Mortimer in his attempt to seize the throne. In the fighting that followed, Percy's son Harry Hotspur was killed, and Percy himself driven into exile in Scotland. From this base he made several more attempts to seize the throne, ending with this action where, with an army of lowland Scots and Northumbrians, he marched on York, intending to take the city. Sir Thomas Rokeby, High Sheriff of Yorkshire, assembled an army to defend the city and they met at Bramham Moor on this date. The result was a rout of the invaders, and Percy himself was killed fighting a rearguard action.

20 FEBRUARY 1925 On returning home from work at the Rowntree chocolate factory on this date, George Taylor arrived at his cottage in New Earswick to find a note from his wife saying, 'Do not think too hard of me, it is all for the best, I cannot go on any longer with this terrible feeling.' Searching the house, Taylor found his wife Edith sitting in the bath in her nightdress, terribly distressed and confused. On the floor of the bathroom lay the lifeless body of their 13-month-old daughter, Betsy. George later told doctors that his wife had been suffering severe depression since the child's birth. Edith was tried for the murder of the child by drowning and was found guilty but insane, and sentenced to be detained in a hospital for treatment. At her trial

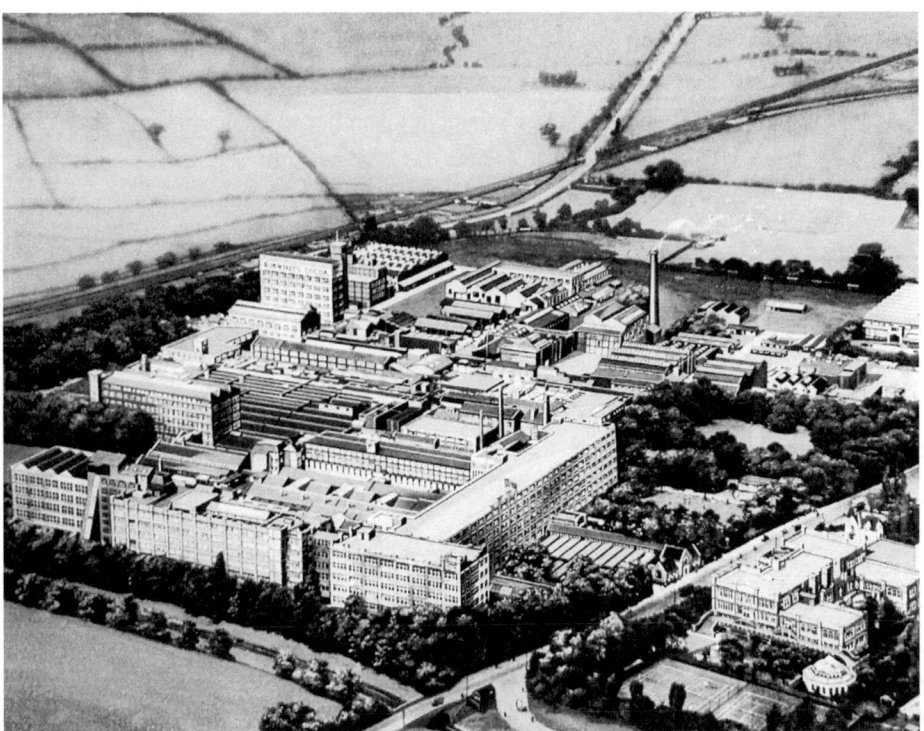

Aerial view of the Rowntree factory, photographed in the 1920s. (Author's collection)

the judge declared that the insanity laws of the country were inadequate, and that it was only because he had used common sense to bend the strict letter of the law that the woman had been saved from the noose.

21 FEBRUARY 1912 Charles Herbert lived in Prospect Street, Fulford, with his wife Minnie and their four children, all aged 5 and under. Herbert worked at the tram depot and, on leaving the house for work on this morning, his wife informed him that she had a premonition that something would happen that day. At around nine o'clock, she went up to a tramcar standing at a nearby terminus, and asked the conductor if he would take a message to her husband, asking him to return home immediately. She then wandered off in the direction of the River Ouse. Herbert received the message and arrived home shortly afterwards. On entering the house, he found all four children lying in bed with cloth handkerchiefs tied tightly around their necks. A doctor was called, who found that two of the children were dead, but he was able to revive the other two. Herbert's wife was nowhere to be found, and it was nearly a month before her body was discovered floating in the river near Selby.

22 FEBRUARY 1877 Charles Burnby, a tinner employed in the Fossgate, was taking some ashes from his place of employment to an ashpit in Black Horse Alley. On opening the door of the pit, he found a green parcel lying on top of the ashes and, taking it up, he opened it to find the dead body of a newborn male child. The police were called and a surgeon examined the body, declaring it to be probably no more than 24 hours old, although fully developed and not born prematurely, and that it had been killed by a great deal of pressure being applied to its head. Inspector Worcester made enquiries to see if he could find any recently pregnant women who were now going about without a baby, but he did not succeed in finding any clues.

Fossgate, photograph taken in 1888. (Author's collection)

23 FEBRUARY 1847 John Fowler, a waggoner from Cawood, a village just south of York, was travelling in the Selby district on his employer's business. At 69 years of age, his mental faculties were failing and he was taken first to the workhouse at Selby, and later to an asylum at Gate Helmsley. Fowler was reported to have behaved in a bizarre manner from first entering the asylum, including refusing to be undressed for bed. He also thrashed his arms about in bed, and an attendant, fearing he would break a window, strapped one of his arms down on the night of the 22nd, although in such a way that he could unbuckle the strap himself. The attendant then secured the door and left. The following morning he found Fowler dead on

the floor of his room, covered in blood, and the door open. In the adjoining room, in which four men were detained, there were marks of blood on the walls and on the clothing of the men, one of whom was found to have a great deal of swelling on his hands. The strap from the bed was also found in that room, and the buckle was broken. It was clear that some violent struggle had taken place during which Fowler had been beaten with the buckle, and had crawled back to his own room to die. However, although the inmate with the swollen hands was clearly involved, it was impossible to tell which of the other men had been, or who had delivered the fatal blows.

24 FEBRUARY 1844 On going to bed at around 11.30 p.m., Mary Ann Musgrave and her husband heard quarrelling from the room below, and then a loud crash of something falling. Afterwards they heard quiet talking but could not make out what was said. The following morning Mary Ann attended the house in question and found her neighbour Alice Bootley lying on the floor at the foot of the bed, and her husband sitting in a corner. William Bootley informed Mary Ann that his wife had fallen and he could not get her to the bed. Alice was insensible and seemed unable to say anything but 'corner, corner'. With the help of her husband and another man, Mrs Musgrave managed to get the woman into her bed and she was attended by a surgeon, who stated that she showed all the symptoms of having suffered a stroke. However, in the neighbourhood others had heard the arguing the night before and suspicion fell on the husband. During the following week – although she never regained the proper power of speech – Mrs Bootley was asked if her husband had done something to her; she pointed to the corner, made a fist and pounded it into her open hand. On the Thursday morning she died, and a post-mortem examination showed marks of what could have been violent injuries, but they all appeared to be old and not recent. An inquest jury had no choice but to find that she had died of natural causes due to a stroke, but suspicion in the local area remained strong that Mr Bootley had done something to bring about her death.

25 FEBRUARY 1953 If you spend any time in York, you are bound to hear the story of Harry Martindale and the Roman soldiers. The event occurred somewhere around this date, although sadly Harry himself doesn't remember the exact day. He was 18 years old at the time and working as an apprentice plumber. On this occasion, he had to go into the cellar of the Treasurer's House next to York Minster to drill a hole in a beam to allow a pipe to go through. Whilst on his ladder he heard a loud horn sound and, turning in the direction from which it came, saw a Roman

legionary walk through the wall followed by around sixteen others. They were tired and dishevelled; marching straight past him and into the opposite wall. They appeared to be walking on their knees, and this made sense as the level of the Roman road would have been around 15in below the cellar floor. Intriguingly, the outfits Harry said they wore made people suspicious, as they did not fit with what was thought at the time to be the proper attire of a Roman soldier. However it was later discovered that auxiliary soldiers in the Roman Army wore outfits and carried weaponry that exactly fitted Harry's description.

The Treasurer's House, where Harry Martindale encountered ghostly Roman soldiers in the basement. (Author's collection)

26 FEBRUARY 1751 At around 4 a.m., York was hit by a storm of hurricane force. Severe damage was described throughout the city, with the roofs of houses being blown away, chimneys being demolished, and trees uprooted. In the countryside around the city, it was said that several houses collapsed under the onslaught. Several people were recorded as having been badly injured, although – miraculously – none were killed. On the north wall of the minster one of the pinnacles and most of the battlements collapsed, and the pinnacle itself fell through the roof and two lofts to come crashing down on to the paved floor beneath. Great damage was also done to the church of All Saints, Pavement, which was described as being 'rent in several places'.

27 FEBRUARY 1808 A report in the *York Herald* of this date details a rather polite incident of highway robbery. Thomas Wales was on his way from Sheriff Hutton to Terrington, near to Castle Howard, when he was approached by two men, one of whom produced a pistol and held it to his breast. They demanded his pocketbook and asked what he had inside. Wales informed them that he had four guinea bills and some shillings in silver. On finding that he had told the truth, the robbers decided to take the four guinea bills, and then returned the pocketbook with the silver still inside and rode off.

28 FEBRUARY 1884 On 28 January of this year, the York police were alerted that a woman in Hungate might have murdered her child. Attending the home to arrest the woman, whose name was Elizabeth Palmer, she was asked by the constable to account for her 2½-year-old son Horatio, and she replied 'it is in the River Ouse, but I did not throw it in'. When asked who did, she replied that it was a woman in Walmgate named Lambert. Palmer was remanded in custody for a week, but with no evidence against her, she was handed over to the workhouse on the grounds of possible insanity. A month later, the body of a child was found in the river at Barlby and identified by Palmer's sister, but at an inquest held on this date, the jury decided that although the body was probably that of Horatio, the evidence was not conclusive.

29 FEBRUARY 1868 Daniel Driscoll was a bricklayer from Tottenham who came north to Yorkshire in search of work. However, having got himself into some form of trouble, he ended up spending some time in prison in Beverley. On this date he was released and set off towards York, again seeking gainful employment, and travelled along with another man released on the same day, by the name of Frederick Parker.

Driscoll had been in possession of a good sum of money – around £4 11s – when imprisoned, and this had been returned to him. Parker, on the other hand, had very little. Along the journey, the two men stopped to drink in two public houses. The second of these was in a village named Bubwith, some distance south of York. This was the last time Driscoll was seen alive. His body was found a few days later in a ditch, with his head caved in using a hedge stake. His money and possessions were missing. Parker was arrested a few days afterwards, after trying unsuccessfully to sell the dead man's pocketwatch. He was executed in York the following month.

MARCH

Stone cross marking the location of the battlefield at Towton,
said to be the bloodiest battle fought on English soil.
(Author's collection)

1 MARCH 1854 John Sayer, a carter said to be an industrious man, went to bed at his home in Walmgate quite early on Shrove Tuesday, having to get up early the next morning for work. His wife had gone out dancing with two women who lodged with them, and the group returned home at around 2 or 3 a.m. on this morning, together with a man named Charles White, a servant. Making a loud racket on their return, the party woke Sayer up, and he complained about the noise, whereupon his wife berated him, telling him that she would show him who was the boss. During this argument, she picked up a broom and began to beat him. He took the stick from her and struck her in return, at which point White called him a coward for striking a woman, and began to punch him. Sayer fell to the ground, and White kicked him once in the side before he and the women departed. The following day, Sayer found himself bruised and short of breath and by the Thursday he was unable to walk. On the following Sunday morning, he died. It was found that his ribs had been broken, and this had caused a slow build up of congestion on his lungs, which was the cause of death. Since it could not be determined which of the pair had struck the fatal blows, both Hannah Sayer and Charles White were charged and convicted of manslaughter.

2 MARCH 1856 Thomas Rylatt went to his work at a gas depot in Monkgate on the night of 1 March, and left his wife Jane at her parents' house. The next morning when he returned to fetch her, her mother told him that Jane was poorly and in bed upstairs. He went to see her and she told him that her head hurt, whereupon he saw some blood behind her ear but she could not tell him how it got there. Later that day when he returned to the house, his mother-in-law told him that his wife was better but asleep, so he went to his home and returned the next day, only to find that she was dead. When he asked how she had got her injury, he was told that she had sat on a chair in front of the coal hole and fallen backwards down the stairs. A doctor, who had been called to see the woman earlier, had arrived shortly after she died, and found her bed to be saturated with blood. Examining the wound, he was quite sure it could not have been caused by a fall. It was at least 2in deep and had nicked the carotid artery, causing the blood loss, convincing him that it could only have been made with a knife. Earlier that day, a neighbour had called at the house and saw the woman's mother holding a knife and threatening her daughter with it. On leaving she had heard the girl cry out, 'Oh, Mother, don't!' The conclusion reached was that her mother had been drinking and had struck the girl, not remembering she had a knife in her hand. She was convicted of manslaughter.

3   **MARCH 1648** The Battle of Seacroft Moor took place close to Leeds on 30 March 1643. It was a victory for the Royalist forces in the English Civil War and around 800 Parliamentarian soldiers were taken captive and brought back to York, where they were housed in the Merchant Adventurers' Hall. According to one of the prisoners named Joseph Bannister, a man named George Clay came and took the names of all the prisoners, and then demanded money for their release. Some paid as much as £60, and Bannister himself was asked for £10, but did not have such a sum. He claimed to have been left in the prison for nineteen weeks, during which time many of those who were also unable to pay died of starvation or cruel use by their captors. During a two-year lull in the war, Bannister decided to prosecute Clay, and on this date was granted a warrant for his arrest by Colonel Lambert. He tracked Clay down to a house in Leeds where Clay, before agreeing to go with him, offered him a cup of ale. Taking the drink, Bannister realised that it had been laced with mercury, and sent for an apothecary, who provided him with a purgative. Clay then offered him 20s to let him go, but Bannister refused and returned him to York and into the custody of Lambert.

The interior of the Merchant Adventurer's Hall, photographed in the 1950s.
Used as a prisoner-of-war camp during the English Civil War. (Author's collection)

4 MARCH 1893 An inquest held on this date heard of the dangers of not seeking proper medical treatment. Mary Wormley, a 50-year-old widow, had been found dead in her house on 18 February, after being ill for some time. She and her husband had been in the habit of seeking treatment for all ills from a herbalist, and when she had started to complain of breathlessness, accompanied by a swelling in her legs, she attended Robert Simpson's establishment to obtain a herbal remedy. Simpson advised her to see a doctor, but she said she could not afford to, and he made her up a remedy, which she took away. Her lodgers state that she became progressively worse from this time on, although she insisted the treatment was making her better. After her death it was found that the remedy contained an infusion of digitalis six times stronger than the recommended dose. The jury at the inquest had no choice but to conclude that this was at the very least a factor in, if not the overall cause of, her death.

5 MARCH 1945 Nunthorpe Grove, a street just outside the city walls in the west of the city, seems to have been the unluckiest place to live in York during the Second World War. The street was badly damaged when several bombs were dropped there during the Baedeker Raid of 1942, during which several residents were badly hurt and one killed. On this night, death rained from the skies once again, but in this case the German Luftwaffe were not to blame. A Royal Canadian Air Force Halifax bomber had taken off from RAF Linton in freezing fog with a full complement of bombs to take part in a raid over Germany. However, the plane had struggled to gain height, and then the flying surfaces began to ice up. The extra weight was too much and the plane broke up over the city, the fuselage falling on to the ill-fated Nunthorpe Grove, destroying five houses, killing five of the residents and injuring eighteen others. One of the engine blocks also crashed through the roof of the kitchens of the nearby Nunthorpe School, although they were unoccupied at the time. All but one of the crew of the aircraft were killed; the wireless operator, however, had a miraculous escape. Bailing out, he was too close to the ground for his parachute to open, but as he approached the ground a fuel tank explosion pushed him sideways, decelerating his fall, and he landed safely on a shed roof, badly hurt but alive.

6 MARCH 1684 The tale of Dick Turpin is told elsewhere in this book. However, his most famous exploit, the moonlight ride, was a fiction invented by novelist William Harrison Ainsworth, but based on a ride made by another highwayman, William 'Swift Nick' Nevison. In 1676, Nevison had robbed a traveller near Gad's Hill in

Plaque commemorating the arrest of William 'Swift Nick' Nevison (here called by the alias John Nevison). (Author's collection)

Kent and, having been seen, escaped across the Thames and galloped the 200-mile journey to York as fast as he could. Arriving just before sunset, he entered into a wager on a bowls match with the Lord Mayor, who was later able to provide an alibi for him in court. Nevison was tried for his crimes on several occasions. In 1677 he was convicted of horse theft at York Assizes, but pardoned after informing against his accomplices. In 1681 he was sentenced to be transported with a company of soldiers to Tangiers, but escaped. He was eventually arrested on this date for the murder of a constable named Darcy Fletcher, at an inn near Wakefield. This time there was no escape: he was brought back to York, and he met his end two months later at the Knavesmire. He is buried in an unmarked grave at St Mary's church in Castlegate.

7 MARCH 1922 The civil court at York Castle heard a case in which an argument between two elderly ladies had escalated into violence. One of the ladies, 73-year-old Mary Ellis, had accused the other lady, a widow of similar age named Edith Stephenson, of sexual improprieties with some soldiers who had recently been stationed near Hunmanby. According to Stephenson, Mrs Ellis had also accused her of having an antisocial disease. She then struck the other woman on the shoulder with a rake. The judge ordered her to pay £2 in damages.

8 MARCH 1650 A deposition was received at York Castle on this day against a group of people believed to be Gypsies. The deposition states that they came to the village of Butterwick and accepted money for telling fortunes. This being shortly after the end of the Civil War, travel around the country was strictly controlled and passes had to be obtained. The party consisted of six women and one man, Richard Smith, who claimed to have such a pass, but this turned out to be forged. He denied the telling of fortunes, and claimed that they had been turned out into the countryside from London after being falsely accused as highway robbers. Nonetheless, the group were sentenced to be hanged, whereupon all of the women claimed to be pregnant. After examination it was found that one of the women, named Barbara Smith, was indeed with child, and as such her life was spared whilst the others were all swiftly despatched.

9 MARCH 1877 A young girl named Margaret Hardiman, an inmate at the women's prison at York Castle, had been set to work washing some of the empty cells, and observed smoke and flames coming from the cell below that in which she was working. Quickly she ran to find a guard. The deputy governor and several officials went to the cell in question and, on opening the door, found the smoke so thick that they could not see inside. The occupant, Ann Griffin, said to be a powerfully built woman, had been in trouble several times in the previous days for smashing windows, and had been set to pick oakum, which she had set alight with the gas lamp in the room and then pressed up against the window frame. As they got the fire under control, Griffin informed the guards that it was her intention to burn the castle to the ground. At her trial, the judge said he looked more harshly on this act than most acts of arson because, had the fire spread, prisoners locked in their cells would have had no chance of escape. He sentenced her to fifteen years' penal servitude.

10 MARCH 1951 The naked and lifeless body of 76-year-old Flora Gilligan was found on the pavement outside of her home in Diamond Street. She had been raped and beaten, and then thrown from an upstairs window to die in the street outside. Fingerprints and footprints were found at the scene, and were found to match those of Private Philip Henry of the King's Own Yorkshire Light Infantry, who was stationed in barracks nearby and had been due to ship out on active duty the following day. He was apprehended and splinters of wood were found about his person that matched the wood from the sill of the window through which she had been ejected. Henry was found guilty and hanged at Leeds three months later.

11 MARCH 1616 Thomas Atkinson, who was executed as a Catholic priest in the city on this date, almost caused a riot even among the Protestant folk of the city, because it was felt that he was condemned unlawfully, there being no proof against him except that he refused to profess that he was not a priest. Under the law, the punishment of execution depended on the court demonstrating that the accused had been ordained a priest overseas after the date when this had been made illegal in England, and that he had returned to England specifically for the purpose of converting others to the Catholic faith, none of which had been shown in court. When Atkinson was confined in York Castle he was put in chains, but the chains continually fell from his legs, which was taken as a sign that God did not approve of his confinement and sentence. In truth it was more likely because of a broken leg he had suffered some time earlier, which had not been set properly.

12 MARCH 1891 Hannah Walls, the keeper of the Crown public house in Holgate Road, appears to have been very determined to take her own life. Having retired to bed around midnight the previous evening, her niece, who was 11 years of age, was awoken by a knocking on the door at around 9 a.m. A neighbour, Mrs Wray, was concerned because she had been expecting to meet with Walls earlier, and the niece also became concerned because her aunt would usually have roused her before this hour. They found her dead on the sofa of a downstairs room; she had used not one but three different methods to end her own life. She had clearly first attempted to hang herself, and the makeshift noose was still around her neck. She had also drunk carbolic acid and then slit her own throat with a razor.

13 MARCH 1896 An inquest was held into the apparent suicide of Arthur Edward Hewison, a solicitor who had been appearing for a client at the York City Court just the day before his death. Hewison was the son of the Revd George Henry Hewison, the vicar of St Denys' church in Walmgate, from a well-known and respected family within the city. His body had been discovered at Clifford Ings, and beside it a

six-chambered pistol with only three chambers loaded. Initial reports suggested that he had placed the pistol in his own mouth and fired, but the inquest found that, whilst he had undoubtedly shot himself, there was insufficient evidence as to whether he had done so deliberately or by accident. He had bought the gun only that morning, and had not owned one before.

14 MARCH 1803 Bizarre scenes occurred on this date at York Castle during the execution of two men, Joseph Heald and John Terry, for the murder of 67-year-old Elizabeth Smith, at the village of Flamshaw. It was well known in the village that Smith had received 18 guineas from her family to purchase a milk cow; the pair had set out to steal this and in the process had beaten the woman to death with a pair of tongs. The men were convicted largely because of Terry's confession, but on the morning of the execution he insisted that Heald had not been involved, and that he had only implicated him because he had been told he might spare his own life that way. As he was led on to the gallows he began shouting out that Heald was innocent, saying, 'don't hang Heald, if you do, I shall be guilty of two murders!' He then attempted to escape, and it eventually took five or six men to drag him to the drop where he continued to struggle, pulling the cap off his head and, at the moment the bolt was released, springing forward and managing to get an arm round part of the railing of the scaffold, holding himself there for about a minute before the executioner could disentangle him and send him to his death. Heald, meanwhile, was said to have accepted his execution with composure, and never attempted to deny his own guilt.

Detail from a broadsheet showing the gallows at the rear of York Castle. (Author's collection)

15 MARCH 1806 Sharp Smith was sentenced to death at the York Assizes for 'taking away one foal and her mare, the property of Daniel Lees'. Smith was just 12 years old at the time of his sentencing. His sentence was later commuted and he was transported overseas.

16 MARCH 1190 Richard I of England, better known as Richard the Lionheart, was crowned on 9 September 1189. At his coronation a deputation of Jews from across the country attended with gifts for the new king but were refused entry and, some reports suggest, were ordered to be whipped. A rumour spread around the country that Richard had ordered the expulsion of the Jews, and anti-Jewish riots started to spread. One of those caught up in this was Benedict of York, who was mortally wounded and died at Northampton while trying to return home. Meanwhile, several noblemen of the city had seen the opportunity to rid themselves of debts to Jewish moneylenders, and one Richard Malebisse raised a mob to attack the property of an agent of Aaron of Lincoln, to whom he was particularly indebted. However, things got out of hand, and the house of Benedict of York was also broken into and his widow and children massacred. Alarmed, one leading Jew, Josce of York, rounded up as much of the Jewish community as he could and they fled to the castle, securing themselves in the keep. The sheriff's troops were called but a stand-off went on for three days. However, the Jews were running out of food and water, and the mob outside were adamant that nobody would be permitted to leave

Plaque dedicated to the Jews who died at Clifford's Tower. (Author's collection)

the tower without first being baptised into the Christian faith. Each morning of the siege, a monk in white robes held Mass at the entrance to the tower, and on the third day he was killed by a falling stone, which only enraged the mob further. Finally, on this date, the rabbi, Yomtob of Joigny, decided that there was only one possible conclusion to the siege; rather than accept baptism, they should take their own lives. In order to save their souls from the mortal sin of suicide, the men were to slit the throats of their wives and children before submitting to Yomtob, who would perform the same action for them. This left the rabbi as the only one to take his own life. Meanwhile, the decision was taken to burn down the wooden keep so that their bodies could not be desecrated after death. Some of the Jews attempted to flee the flames rather than submit to Yomtob's instruction, but were captured by the mob and put to death anyway. Estimates put the numbers of those who died at around 150, and afterwards the mob marched to the minster, where the records of debts were kept and compelled the guardians to turn these records over to them so they could be burned. An inquest was later held, and while the constable and sheriff of the city were dismissed and Richard Malebisse had some property confiscated, none of those involved in the mob were ever prosecuted.

17 MARCH 1809 The crimes of Mary Bateman, the famous 'Yorkshire Witch', occurred mostly in Leeds, but it was to York that she was conducted for her trial on this date. She was found guilty of the murder of Rebecca Perigo by poisoning, an act she had carried out as part of a campaign where she had robbed Perigo and her husband of over £70 worth of goods under the pretence of lifting a curse from them. Far from being actually well versed in the ways of the 'wise woman', Bateman was an accomplished con artist whose crimes had cut a swathe through Yorkshire over the previous years, but she wasn't finished yet. At her trial, she was sentenced to death, and when asked whether she had anything to say, replied that she couldn't be hanged as she was twenty-two weeks pregnant. The judge ordered her examination by a midwife, but such was Bateman's reputation that none would come. Eventually he empanelled twelve middle-aged married women to examine her in the closed-off courtroom. After an hour they called the court back in and announced the whole thing to be a lie.

Mary Bateman, the Yorkshire Witch. (Author's collection)

18   MARCH 1471 Although a grim event only in terms of what was soon to come, on this date York opened its gates to the armies of King Edward IV and allowed them inside. Edward had ridden into York in triumph after the Battle of Towton ten years earlier; this time he entered as the head of an invading army, having been deposed from the throne by his former friend Richard Neville and through the treachery of his brother George. The latter had hoped to take the throne for himself, but his ambitions had been thwarted and the feeble King Henry VI was restored. George had made approaches to

Edward IV.

Edward in his exile in Burgundy to return to the York fold. Now Edward had returned, along with their other brother Richard of Gloucester (later Richard III), and needed a base from which to strike south. He had been turned away at Cromer, and again at Kingston-Upon-Hull, but York welcomed him, possibly due to the high regard in which Gloucester had always been held there, and based on his assurances that he had come only to reclaim his fiefdom. Within two months Neville was dead at the Battle of Barnet, Henry's son and heir Edward was killed at Tewkesbury, and Henry himself had died, officially of 'melancholy' but almost certainly murdered on Edward's orders and possibly by Gloucester himself.

19   MARCH 1891 An altercation in a stable led to a rather unusual court case. Robert Greaves was attempting to sue John Hollidge, the owner of the stables, for £20 damages for assaulting him. According to Greaves, he had gone to the stables to view a pony that he believed belonged to him, but as soon as he arrived, Hollidge assaulted him and beat him with his fists and a stick. Hollidge, on the other hand, stated that Greaves had simply entered his stables for no reason whatsoever and refused to leave. He also suggested that the man was extremely drunk at the time. Finally losing patience, he had attempted to push him out of the door, at which point Greaves had attacked him violently and he had been forced to defend himself. As his story seemed to be borne out by the witnesses, the judge ruled in favour of Hollidge and ordered Greaves to pay costs (although Greaves claimed to have a witness of his own who he said was in America). In summing up, the judge declared that in going to another man's premises, refusing to leave, and assaulting Hollidge, any injuries he had sustained were no more than he deserved.

20 MARCH 1776 Elizabeth Boardingham became the last person to be burned alive at the stake in Yorkshire. Boardingham's husband John was an abusive petty criminal who had treated her badly and, as a result, she had begun a relationship with another man, Thomas Ainkey. After three months she returned to her husband, but persuaded Ainkey that she could no longer stand to be under his control. On the night of 13 February, Ainkey had come to their house and stabbed John twice before fleeing the scene, leaving the knife still in the body. John died the next day and the pair were both arrested. Ainkey was hanged for murder, but Boardingham was tried for the crime of 'petty treason', which was a standard offence for a wife killing her husband, and carried the standard sentence of burning. In fact, before her execution, a rope was placed around her neck, and as the wood beneath her started to burn it was pulled tight in order that she would asphyxiate and be spared the flames.

21 MARCH 867 This is the date given for the death of King Aelle of Northumbria at the hands of Ivar the Boneless and Halfdan Ragnarsson, the Viking leaders of the Great Heathen Army, in revenge for the killing of their father Ragnar Lodbrok. York had been sacked by the Viking army six months earlier, but Aelle was absent at the time, and so they returned on this date in great force. Some contemporary accounts state that a fleet of longboats 2 miles long arrived in the city via the River Ouse, and that Aelle and the former Northumbrian king, Osberht, were killed in the battle. According to the Viking sagas, however, Aelle was executed by the method known as the blood eagle. A particularly hideous form of death, this would have involved his back being sliced open and his ribs cut away, following which his lungs would be pulled out through the opening so that his last dying breaths would cause them to inflate and deflate outside his body like flapping wings.

22 MARCH 1602 The execution of James Harrison as a Catholic priest in York on this date seems to have come as something of a surprise to the victim. He had been sentenced at the Lent Assizes, along with a lay gentleman named Anthony Batty or Bates who had been accused of harbouring him. However, at his trial the judges set aside the decision of the date of his execution until another date, and then left town without giving their decision. As such, when he was told on the night of the 21st that he was to die the following morning he was taken unawares, but very quickly recovered his countenance and sat down to eat his supper, telling the steward of the prison 'let us eat and drink, for tomorrow we shall die'. After his execution, his head was later smuggled to an English Franciscan monastery in Douay in France, where it was kept in the altar as a relic.

23 MARCH 1317 The date of the final battle of Sir Gosselin Danville is not known but it was sometime around this date. Sir Gosselin was a notorious character in medieval England as a nobleman who had inherited a vast fortune and squandered it all on drinking, gambling and whoring. Finding himself broke and unable to continue his lavish lifestyle, he had resolved on a career of highway robbery and, having access to the higher echelons of society, he was privy to when the richest prey would be on the roads and vulnerable. So lucrative were his raids that he raised a veritable army of outlaws to accompany him, and on one infamous occasion they robbed King Edward II and his party. The band of brigands regularly met at an inn close to York where Sir Gosselin had begun an affair with the landlord's wife, and when the man became wise to this betrayal he informed the Sheriff of Yorkshire of the nobleman's whereabouts. The sheriff, apprehensive of the knight's reputation, put together a posse of 600 men to arrest him, and a pitched battle ensued during which it is said that a third of the sheriff's men were killed. Sir Gosselin and twenty-three of his comrades were captured and escorted back to York, where the sheriff had them summarily executed without trial.

24 MARCH 1570 The Rising of the North was an attempt by northern earls faithful to the Catholic Church to remove Elizabeth I from the throne and replace her with Mary, Queen of Scots. Led by Charles Neville, 6th Earl of Westmorland and Thomas Percy, 7th Earl of Northumberland, it began in November 1569, but petered out after they met strong opposition the following year. The rebels mostly fled to Scotland but many were captured along the way. Among these were Simon Digby, John Fulthorpe, Robert Pennyman and Thomas Bishop, who were conducted to York Castle and imprisoned there. On this date they suffered punishment by being hanged, drawn and quartered at the Knavesmire. Their heads were then displayed, one on each of the four main city gates of York, and their bodies similarly displayed (one quarter at each gate), as a warning to all of the consequences of standing against the monarch.

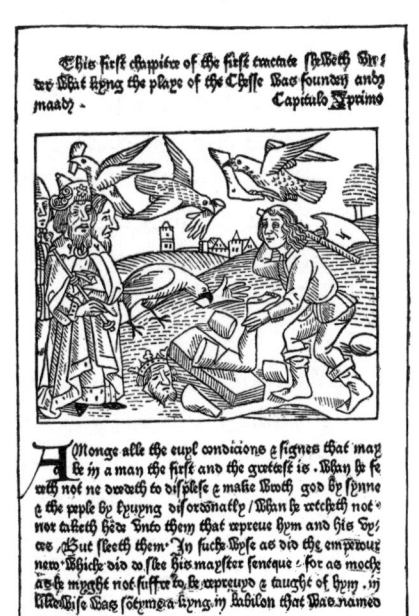

Contemporary pamphlet. (Author's collection)

25 MARCH 1586 Saint Margaret Clitherow was the wife of a butcher who lived in York's most famous street, The Shambles. Born Margaret Middleton, she grew up in a Protestant family but converted to Catholicism at the age of 18. This was during the reign of Queen Elizabeth I, when the Catholic faith had been driven underground. Although a Protestant himself, Margaret's husband John, whom she married at age 15, was accepting of her religion and allowed her to conduct services in their house as well as provide an escape route for priests in the attic. She was arrested in 1586 and tried for the crime of harbouring priests, but refused to plead in order to prevent a trial in

Martyrdom of St Margaret Clitherow. (Author's collection)

which her children would be forced to testify under threat of torture. As a result, on this date, she underwent the standard punishment for this refusal – being crushed to death. She was taken to the Ouse Bridge, where she was stripped naked and laid over a sharp rock. Her own front door was then laid on top of her and slowly loaded up with heavy rocks. This would have caused her spine to snap over the sharp rock and her ribs to start breaking. Her lungs would then be punctured and collapse, causing her to suffocate to death. After Margaret's death, her hand was removed to a reliquary and now resides in the Bar Convent in York. She was canonised in 1970 by Pope Paul VI.

26 MARCH 1743 An incident of highway robbery involving one John Kirton, a carpenter of York, who was returning to the city with a considerable sum of money said to be £446, occurred on this date. At some time between 4 and 5 p.m., Kirton was set upon by a 'single highwayman' who the *York Courant* described as 'well mounted'. Kirton attempted to resist and escape, whereupon his attacker 'used him very barbarously, cut open his bags, cut his bridle, and also his stirrups and the girdle of his saddle, and after giving him several strokes with an oaken stick, left him for dead'. Kirton managed to recover enough to raise the alarm, and many from the locality set out to search for the culprit, but he was able to get away unapprehended.

27 MARCH 1634 A wandering minstrel by the name of John Bartendale was hanged at the Knavesmire for a felony crime, the nature of which is not recorded. Bartendale remained suspended from the noose for some time before being taken down and buried close to the gallows. Later that day, a Mr Vavasours was riding past the grave when he saw the earth move and called on his servant to help him uncover what might be there. In doing so, they found Bartendale still very much alive beneath the soil. He was taken back to York Castle where, at the next assizes, he was tried again, but his survival was seen as a sign of his innocence and he was given a full and free pardon. He is said to have lived a good and blameless life from then on.

28 MARCH 1757 This is the date of execution for Mary Ellah, who was tried and found guilty of petty larceny, or the murder of a husband by a wife. Accounts differ as to how this act was carried out, with some reports stating that she strangled him, but the majority opinion seems to have been that she struck him on the temple with an axe. She was to be punished by being burned at the stake on the Knavesmire at York, but she was in fact hanged first, before her body was taken down from the gallows and burned.

29 MARCH 1731 Very few details are available for the crime of Benjamin Armitt, who was hanged at the Knavesmire, having been tried and found guilty of murder at York Castle. What is known is that the man lived in Hemingbrough, a little way south of the city, and that the victim was Thomas Laird, his serving boy. Laird had in some way failed in his duties, for which Armitt had chosen to administer a whipping so severe that the boy never recovered, dying shortly afterwards. Armitt's defence was that he had not intended to kill the boy, but merely to provide 'correction'.

30 MARCH 1461 The Battle of Towton took place around 12 miles outside York to the south-west on 29 March. It is considered, to this day, to be one of the bloodiest battles ever to take place on English soil. The decisive battle of the first phase of the Wars of the Roses, it was fought between the Yorkist claimant to the throne, Edward of March, and forces loyal to the Lancastrian King Henry VI. Some 75,000 took to the field, and around 28,000 died. At the end of the battle it is said that the ground was no longer visible beneath the bodies of the dead, and the

Henry VI.

The Bloody Meadow. This was the location where the fiercest hand-to-hand fighting of the Battle of Towton occurred. The name is said to derive from the fact that so much blood soaked into the ground here that the Cock Beck, the stream the passes through the meadow, ran red for days afterwards. (Author's collection)

blood that ran away through the Cock Beck, which crossed the battlefield, turned the waters of the River Wharfe, into which it ran, bright red. On this date, Edward rode in triumph through the Micklegate Bar beneath the heads of his father and brother, which still adorned the gate following the Battle of Wakefield. Edward had them taken down and reunited with their bodies for a decent Christian burial, before executing all those involved in their deaths and mounting those heads in their place.

31 MARCH 1379 On 1 March, at a special meeting in York, it had been decided that a new place of execution should be chosen for the city, and the place chosen was the Knavesmire, where a three-legged gallows began construction seven days later. Known locally as Tyburn after the similar gallows at Marble Arch in London, these gallows were first used on this date to hang one Edward Hewison, who had been convicted of raping 22-year-old Louisa Bentley in a field in Sheriff Hutton Road. After his execution, Hewison's body was taken back to the location of the crime and hung in chains from a gibbet. The Knavesmire remained York's place of execution until 1801.

APRIL

The grave of Dick Turpin. (Author's collection)

1 APRIL 1670 Mary Earnley, a young girl who lived with her father in the village of Alne, just outside York, fell into a fit on this day which lasted for over an hour, during which she continually cried out that a woman named Anne Wilkinson was pricking her on her thighs and about her body with pins. The girl's father called for Wilkinson to come to the house, and as she entered the young girl cried out 'that is she!' and 'burn her, burn her, she tormented two of my sisters'. Earnley had, indeed, had two sisters who had both died during the previous year, and according to a woman named Anne Mattson, a black ribbon with a crooked pin in the end had been found in the mouth of one of them after death. Wilkinson denied any bewitching of the Earnley girls, and said she had been sitting in a chair before her fire all morning. She was charged with witchcraft, but later found not guilty by the York Assizes.

2 APRIL 1896 An inquest was held this day on the body of a man named Arthur Lolley, which had been found in a yard behind the Lord Nelson Inn on Walmgate. Lolley had died either the previous day or the day before that, and had last been seen at the Three Cups Inn in Fossbridge in the company of a person known as Scotch Annie. This was about 9.30 p.m. on the evening of 31 March, and the following day Thomas Emms passed through the yard behind the Lord Nelson Inn and saw someone lying in the gutter. Thinking them drunk and asleep, he paid no attention, but found that he was still there later in the day when he returned to his home, and at that point inspected the body and found that the man was dead. His mouth and stomach were found to be filled with mud, and it was therefore presumed that he had suffocated while lying face downwards. Scotch Annie was identified as being a woman named Annie Campbell, who admitted that she had been with Lolley, but stated that both were so drunk that she had no memory of the events of the night in question.

3 APRIL 1595 Of the many executed for their Catholic faith in York, Henry Walpole seems to have been the most unfortunate. Born in Norfolk and educated both at Oxford and Cambridge, Walpole travelled to France, where he was ordained in 1592 and sent to Italy to take holy orders. He then travelled to Flanders where he was captured by Calvinists and imprisoned for a year. On his release he asked to be allowed to travel to England, but instead was sent to Spain where, after some service, the king sent him back to Flanders to set up a seminary. Finally, after completing this work, he was given permission to travel to England. He arrived on 4 December 1593 and within less than twenty-four hours had been apprehended and taken to York Castle. After being examined by the Council of the North, he languished in prison at the castle until February when he was sent to London, where he was detained in the Tower of London and, over the course of the next year, tortured no less than fourteen times to obtain information about Catholic activities in England. Finally he was sent back to York to stand trial and was convicted on this date. Four days later he was drawn on a hurdle to the Knavesmire in the company of another Catholic priest, Alexander Rawlins. Because the two men attempted to give comfort to one another, their captors insisted on tying them facing in opposite directions so that one man's feet were beside the other's head. He was made to watch Rawlins' execution, which included hanging, disembowelment and dissection, all the while being told he would be spared the same fate if he would proclaim the queen's supremacy over the Church. Adamantly refusing, he submitted to the noose and began to recite the Angelus prayer, whereupon he was hanged with the words still in his mouth.

4 APRIL 1879 Margaret Douglas, the wife of a coach painter in Tanner's Moat, died in the hospital in York on this date after lingering for a day following an attempt at both murder and suicide. The previous morning, a neighbour had entered the house and found Douglas' daughter Lucy in a distressed condition. Alarmed, she ran upstairs to alert the mother, and found her lying across the floor in a pool of blood with her throat cut and a table knife alongside her. She was not dead, so the woman went to fetch a Dr Stephens, who treated the woman and also discovered that Lucy had been poisoned with something her mother had given her in a cup. The girl was given an emetic and she quickly recovered. On a slate in the kitchen, Mrs Douglas had written that she wished to die and hoped God would forgive her. Her eldest son had been recently sent to prison for stealing £70 from his place of business, and another of their children had died a few weeks before; it was believed that it was the combination of these two events that had sent her into a depression.

5 APRIL 1861 A report that gives an interesting insight into mortality in Victorian York was published on this date. Dividing the city into three sections, centred on Walmgate, Bootham and Micklegate, it quickly becomes apparent that mortality ran at a much higher rate in the first of these, and was lowest in the last. This, of course, follows the pattern of housing: the Walmgate area contained most of the poorer and slum districts, while Micklegate contained the middle-class districts to the west of the city. The data in the report covered a twenty-two-year period from 1838 to 1859. In Walmgate and Bootham, the major cause of death was zymotic diseases, including smallpox, typhus and scarlet fever. In Walmgate, diarrhoea was also a significant factor. Meanwhile, suicide was also much more prevalent in Walmgate, accounting for nearly twice as many deaths as in Bootham, and around eight times as many as

The Bedern Hall. (Author's collection)

in Micklegate. Life expentancy was significantly different, people living on average for ten years longer in Micklegate than in Walmgate, with Bootham falling somewhere in the middle. It was pointed out that the figures for Bootham were skewed by the inclusion in that district of the Bedern, generally considered the worst slum in York for most of the nineteenth century.

6 APRIL 1745 Abraham Dealtry was convicted of having carried out a highway robbery against a Susannah Shackleton, and had been sentenced to death. His execution was due to be carried out on this date and accordingly he was taken to the Knavesmire where, after the usual preliminaries, the rope was placed around his neck and he was hanged. Having hung for around ten minutes, Abraham's body was cut down and put into a coffin by his friends, who had arranged to have him buried in the Trinity churchyard. Taking him to a house in Trinity Lane and preparing him

7   **APRIL   1739**   The notorious highwayman Richard 'Dick' Turpin was executed on the Knavesmire of York. Originally born in Essex, Turpin had arrived in Yorkshire on the run after committing a murder in Epping Forest, and almost certainly this was not his only unlawful killing. He was actually arrested for killing a gamecock belonging to another gentleman in a street in Brough, and from there incarcerated in Beverley before being moved to the Castle Gaol in York when it became clear that he was not a horse trader named John Palmer, as he claimed, and he was convicted of the theft of three horses. His real identity was discovered when a letter to his brother-in-law was intercepted. Although in reality a brutal man with a disfigured face due to a bout of smallpox in his youth, Turpin was cast, in Victorian times, as a romanticised gentleman of the road and has remained as such to this day. Much of this has its roots in his flamboyant behaviour on the gallows. Having been transported to his execution by cart, waving and joking with the crowd on the journey, he is said to have climbed on to the gallows, placed the noose around his own neck and leapt off without waiting for the hangman to do his duty. Witnesses suggested that Turpin's leg trembled just before his final leap, and it may have been that he was acting with false bravado and jumped when he realised his nerve might not hold much longer.

Frontispiece for a near contemporary account of the trial of Dick Turpin. (Author's collection)

8 APRIL 1902 A young girl died early on this morning in York County Hospital, having apparently taken her own life by drinking carbolic acid. The story that emerged regarding Eva Ruddock was filled with tragedy. Her parents had turned her out of the house some time before, after a lodger complained that some of his money was missing, and she went into service with a local parson, whereupon her mother wrote to the parson telling him of the theft and she was dismissed. The girl had a number of debts she was struggling to pay, which is why she was supposed to be the culprit. She had been engaged to a young man named Isaac Dew – who she had been seeing for two years – and had recently fallen pregnant. He promised to marry her if she paid off her debts and said that he would help. However, he later seems to have gone back on his word, and the girl was soon living with a couple called the Wheatleys. On the night of 28 March, she had attempted to kill herself by drinking laudanum at their house and the couple, along with Dew, provided an emetic to save her. On the night before her death she had gone to her mother's house and was found lying in the yard with the carbolic acid bottle beside her. Rather than help her, her mother had turned her out of the house and called the police, telling them only that she was drunk. When they arrived, the girl was unconscious in the street outside and rushed to the hospital, but she lingered only a few hours. Such was the public feeling that crowds gathered at her funeral to jeer and shout abuse at Dew and the family members, and her mother was unable to attend due to threats that had been made against her. At the inquest, the coroner returned a verdict of suicide, but added a public censure to her family, and particularly the mother, saying that they had greatly contributed to a state of mind that had brought about her death.

9 APRIL 1842 Jonathan Taylor had been a tenant farmer in Escrick until he took up with a woman he had met in York who was half his age, and left his wife to go and live with her in Hull. A few years later, his new paramour had tired of him and he returned to the family, by which time his son had taken the tenancy of the farm and allowed him to live in the house but nothing more. His wife, Ellen, had become accustomed to looking after the money of the household, and the sale of some cattle had brought in a great deal. Taylor asked her for some of this money but was refused. The following morning the family had gone out to work in the fields, leaving their mother alone in the house, or so they thought. However, it is believed that Taylor had secreted himself somewhere, and when they returned they found their mother dead, apparently burned to death after her clothes had caught fire. Doctors were called and an examination found ligature marks, which suggested that she had been strangled before being burned. Suspicion naturally fell on Taylor, especially as the money which his wife had been seen placing in a drawer the day before had now gone. He was found guilty of her murder at the York Assizes and executed on this date.

10 APRIL 1752 Two men were hanged at the gallows on the Knavesmire on this day on a charge of housebreaking. The names of the men were Robert Loveday and Benjamin Farmery, and as they were brought to the place of execution they were asked, as was the custom, if they had any last words to say before their sentence was carried out. Farmery is said to have behaved penitently, giving a statement of his regret and asking for the Lord's forgiveness. Loveday, on the other hand, simply asked if he might have a last pipe of tobacco. Among those who had gathered to witness the execution, one was found who was willing to supply him with such, and so it was provided to him. As soon as it was placed in his mouth and lit, he quickly pulled the noose over his own neck and, possibly in imitation of Dick Turpin's actions thirteen years earlier, leaped from the cart to his doom.

11 APRIL 1733 Elizabeth Umpleby, a young woman from a good family in Wighill, near Tadcaster, had enjoyed a dalliance with a man named John Addinell, and had fallen pregnant as a result. Addinell had promised that he would make an honest woman of her before the child was born but, presumably in hope that she would not carry to term and he would be released from that promise, he continually procrastinated. As the time of her confinement came near, on this date she demanded that he carry through on his promise, and produced an envelope of poison that she said she would take if he refused. However, the young man remained obstinate, and as a result the girl swallowed the poison and died the following morning.

12 APRIL 627 On this date Edwin, the Anglo-Saxon King of Northumbria, was baptised in a new church built on the spot where York Minster stands today, in fulfilment of a promise made to the monk Paulinus. A year earlier Chwichelm, the King of the West-Saxons, had sent an assassin named Eamer to the city, then known as Eoforwic. Eamer had killed two of Edwin's court, Lilla and Forthere, and wounded the king himself before being put to death. On that very same night, Edwin's wife Aethelberg, a devout Christian who had brought Paulinus to the city, gave birth to a daughter, Eanfleda. Edwin went to Paulinus and offered Eanfleda to God if Paulinus would procure the hand of God to strike down Chwichelm. In the war that followed, Edwin was victorious, slaying Chwichelm and four other royal personages of the West-Saxons, and devastating their army. On his return, he ordered the construction of the church, dedicated to St Peter, and also proclaimed Paulinus as the first Archbishop of York.

York Minster at night. (© Darren Finders)

13 **APRIL 1642** Edmund Catherick learned the hard way that you can choose your friends, but you can't choose your family. Arrested under suspicion of being a Catholic priest, he asked for the aid of a magistrate, Justice Dodsworth, a relative through marriage. Dodsworth instead used the admissions Catherick had made to him in private as evidence to convict him, and he was sentenced to death. He was condemned along with another man, John Lockwood, who had remarkably managed to survive as a Catholic priest for over forty years despite the fierce repression of the establishment. He had been tried twice before, the first time resulting in exile, and on the second he was condemned to death but later reprieved. Lockwood was now in his late eighties, an impressive age for a man to reach at that time. Both men initially received a stay of execution, but were hanged, drawn and quartered at this date at the King's Manor. King Charles I, recently arrived in York after breaking with Parliament in London, attended the execution personally.

The doorway of the King's Manor, photographed in the late nineteenth century. (Author's collection)

14 **APRIL 1821** Hangman William Curry was employed on this day to carry out two executions in different parts of the city. The first, at York Castle, went without a hitch but, having decided to walk to York City Gaol at Baile Hill for the second, he was roundly abused by locals throughout the walk. Stopping to fortify his nerves with strong drink at regular intervals, he arrived at his second appointment clearly inebriated and had trouble placing the noose around the condemned man's neck. As the crowd jeered at him, he brandished the rope in their direction, shouting 'some of you come up, and I'll try it!' Eventually the governor of the gaol had to step in and call for calm before instructing two of his assistants to aid Curry in getting the job finished.

15 **APRIL 1944** RAF Dishforth is an airfield a short distance north of York. On this night, a Halifax EB205 bomber aircraft was sent on a routine training mission, but on returning to the base around 11 p.m., the crew found the area enshrouded in a heavy storm. They were given priority landing clearance and began their descent

through the cloud that was only at around 500ft. However, they found that they had overshot and, unable to ascend through the cloud to make another approach, decided to put down instead at a civilian aerodrome at Topcliffe nearby. But the runway at Topcliffe was shorter and the aircraft careered off the end and into some nearby railway cottages. Five of the crew, two occupants of one of the cottages, and a cyclist who happened to be passing, were all killed. One of the two surviving crew members, gunner John Tynski, came to in the midst of the burning wreckage and, risking his own life, gathered up the ammunition from the aircraft and moved it away from the fire to prevent explosions.

16 APRIL 1570 Baptism records in the church of St Michael le Belfry show that one of York's most notorious residents received his christening there on this date. Born in the Stonegate area probably around three days earlier, the still extant records give his name as Guy Fawkes. He attended St Peter's School in the city and, although born into a prominent Protestant family, is believed to have been converted to Catholicism by John Pulleyn, the headmaster of that school. Fawkes became infamous for his part in the plot to assassinate King James I by blowing up the Houses of Parliament. Put to death on 31 January 1606, he was sentenced to first be drawn to his execution behind

The Gunpowder Plot conspirators. Guy Fawkes is third from the right.

a horse, with his head close to the ground. His genitals were to be cut off and burned before his eyes before he was hanged, his heart and bowels removed and burned, his head displayed on a pike for a year, and his body quartered. It was probably a mercy that he was spared all but the first part of this punishment when he either jumped or fell from the gallows and broke his neck, so that by the time of his actual hanging he was already dead.

17 APRIL 1790 One night in August 1789, five button manufacturers in Sheffield stopped at a public house for a beer on their way home from work. One of the men, John Wharton, had to leave to perform some errands and, intending to return, left behind a basket containing some mutton and other goods. For a joke, the men ate the mutton and hid the basket, although they clubbed together the money to pay for the consumed meat. Unfortunately, Wharton did not return that night, and when he later found that his basket had been stolen by the men, he reported them to the police and they were arrested. Taken to York, they were tried and convicted of robbery and sentenced to death. One of the men, Michael Bingham, was acquitted as merely a bystander, and another, John Booth, had his sentence commuted to transportation, but the remaining two, John Stevens and Thomas Lastley, were due for execution on this date. On the arrival in Sheffield of this news, a petition was got up and signed by many prominent citizens attesting that the whole affair was a mistake and pleading for a reprieve. The petition was sent to London and an unconditional pardon was granted. Unfortunately there were delays on the roads, and the pardon did not arrive in York until the 19th, by which time the men had been dead for two days.

18 APRIL 1902 In a field just outside York, a dreadful discovery was made on this date. The bodies of a young couple were discovered, both with their throats slit, with an open razor near the hand of the young man. The girl had a silk scarf tied around her eyes as a blindfold, and appeared to have been compliant in her own death. The man's clothing was saturated with water. The scene suggested that the pair had made a suicide pact; the man had slit the girl's throat before attempting to drown himself and, discovering he could not, had chosen to use the razor on himself instead. They were discovered to be Lewis Carter and Kate Bray from Huddersfield. They had been engaged to be married, until her father had discovered that Carter already had a wife, and had therefore ordered his daughter to break off with the man. They had disappeared four days earlier, after she had received a telegram telling her to meet him in Leeds.

19 APRIL 1890 The body of a 5-month-old girl was found floating in the River Ouse on this date. According to the coroner's report, it had been in the river for probably twenty days, and death had occurred due to pressure on the pit of the stomach and liver, so the child may have been dead when she was put in the water. The body was found to be the daughter of a servant girl, Elizabeth Sanderson, who lived at Sand Hutton near York, and Charles Haggard, an engine fireman in the city. Born out of wedlock, Haggard had been paying the child's mother 2s a week for the baby's upkeep, but she had met with him and told him she was sending the girl to her aunt in Market Weighton and if he would pay her 12s 6d to pay the travel expenses, he would have to pay no more afterwards. He did so, and a few weeks later she told him the child had died of a severe cold. The child's nursemaid stated that Sanderson had asked her for a coat to wrap around the child so she could take it to her aunt. Later that afternoon she had seen the woman without the child, and with the coat over her arm. At her trial the jury acquitted her, stating that they believed she had killed the child, but did not feel they had enough evidence that she had done so intentionally.

20 APRIL 1907 In a story that will be related in the entry for 2 May, a soldier named Barker was sentenced to five years in prison for the manslaughter of his wife, whom he believed to be having an affair with a man named Childs. Barker served over three and a half years of his sentence, and was released on good behaviour on this date. Returning to his home in York, Barker retrieved a carving knife from his kitchen, and then went out into the city searching for Childs, eventually finding the man in a public house. Confronting his enemy, he attempted to drive the knife into the other man's face, but was prevented from doing so by the other patrons of the establishment, although Childs did suffer a bad cut above the eye. Barker was returned to prison to serve out the rest of his sentence, and was additionally bound over on condition that on his release he did not return to York.

21 APRIL 1868 Richard Leaf, a tailor from Bishopthorpe, was at the Woodman's Arms in that village on this afternoon and also inside drinking were a number of navvies from the nearby railway works, some of whom lodged at his house. According to the proprietor, Leaf had drunk two whiskies, but was not intoxicated, although the navvies had consumed considerably more. One of the navvies set upon another, who appeared reluctant to quarrel, and Leaf stepped in to defend the man, which resulted in a fight during which he was punched in the face before the proprietor stepped in to stop things. Later he complained of having a headache, and set off for home. A while

later, a young girl coming home from school discovered him laid out on the road outside. He was carried back inside but was found to be dead. His face was severely bruised and blood was flowing from his nose, although it was believed that this latter was caused by his striking his face as he fell. An inquest was unable to tell whether his death was caused by the blow to the face or not.

22 APRIL 1644 At the beginning of the English Civil War, York remained loyal to King Charles I and became one of his major staging posts, as well as hosting a propaganda office. As such, it was a strategic position, and on this date a Scottish Covenanter army under the Earl of Leven and the Parliamentarian army of Sir Thomas Fairfax approached the city from different directions and placed it under siege. The Marquess of Newcastle, who then held the city for the Royalists, sent his cavalry out at the last minute to join up with other Royalist forces and then set about defending the city with mostly foot soldiers. The Siege of York lasted for close to three months, ending on 16 July with the surrender of the city on easy terms.

King Charles I.

23 APRIL 1684 This being St George's Day, a cannon salute was fired from the roof of Clifford's Tower, the central bailey tower of York Castle, which was now essentially being used only to store gunpowder and shot. According to the official explanation, this salute somehow caused woodwork in the castle to catch fire, and this fire travelled down through the woodwork until it found the magazine and the gunpowder ignited. The resulting explosion blew the roof from the tower and gutted the interior, the condition it remains in to this day. By the time of the explosion, the 'mince pie', as it was known locally due to its appearance, had become deeply unpopular with both the troops and the local populace, its upkeep was a drain on city finances and its potential demolition was regularly toasted before the incident. The fact that nobody was hurt in the explosion, and that members of the garrison appear to have removed all their private belongings shortly before the incident, have led to speculation that the explosion may not have been as accidental as was claimed.

Eighteenth-century engraving of York from the River Ouse, showing the castle and Clifford's Tower in the foreground. (Author's collection)

24 APRIL, 1851 Today saw the conclusion of a lengthy inquest – which had begun five days earlier – into the death of James Flannery. The affair started on the night of the 16th, when a man named Patrick Jordan had had words with three brothers – James, Michael and Henry Donallin – about some suggestion they had made regarding his wife's behaviour. The following morning, Michael and Henry had entered Jordan's yard armed with stones and challenged anyone to fight them. Meanwhile, James Donallin had found Jordan's wife in the street and struck her in the face, causing a black eye. Flannery, who was the woman's father, went out to have words with them, but accused Henry of the deed, and while they were arguing, James went inside and collected a long-handled brush, returned and knocked Flannery to the ground with it. Michael is then said to have struck the man across the head with a flagstone. He fell unconscious, and was carried indoors where he lingered for two days before dying of the injury. Michael Donallin was charged with manslaughter, and James with aiding and abetting. Insufficient evidence was found against Henry to charge him. James was later acquitted, but Michael was given three months' hard labour after pleading guilty.

25 APRIL, 1845 A fight between two youths in the Bedern on this date ended in death. George Lazenby, just 8 years old, was hanging around with a group of boys in the alley, one of whom was 13-year-old William Wilkinson. It seems that Lazenby was taunting the older boy in some way and Wilkinson, losing patience, turned around, picked the younger boy up and threw him to the ground, where he hit his head on the flagstones. Running home crying, Lazenby complained to his mother of head pains, then began to vomit uncontrollably. His mother rushed him to the local chemist's shop, where the owner examined the boy and suggested that he needed to be taken to a hospital. By the time he arrived he was said to be almost comatose, and died later that night.

26 APRIL 1154 William Fitzherbert was twice Archbishop of York, having first taken office in 1141 and then being deposed by Cistercians opposed to his tenure in 1147. Nonetheless, he was popular with the city folk, and on the death of his successor he travelled to Rome to plead with the Pope for reinstatement. His appointment was

Statue of William Fitzherbert, Archbishop of York on two occasions, canonised as St William of York. (Author's collection)

Tomb of St William of York. (Author's collection)

confirmed on 20 December 1153, and he set off to travel back to York in triumph. The exact date of his arrival is not known, but it was close to this date. Most of the population gathered on the Ouse Bridge to cheer him into the city. The bridge had been constructed from wood during the Viking times some 200 years earlier and sadly the weight of the crowd was more than it could take. It collapsed, plunging most of them into the river. William is said to have fallen to his knees and prayed for their deliverance and, miraculously, nobody died. Largely as a result of this miracle, and others related to his grave in York Minster, he was canonised as St William of York in 1227.

27 APRIL 1876 Reports in several newspapers of this date tell of a girl named Louisa Driffield who lived in Haxby on the outskirts of York and had been recently apprehended by police. Neighbours had, for some time, been suspicious that she might be with child, and when she disappeared from the village it was rumoured that she had gone away to be delivered of the baby. However, a few days later she returned without it, but also showing a remarkable loss of girth. When challenged, she strenuously denied that she had been pregnant and her parents insisted likewise, but eventually the story reached the ears of Superintendent Hunter of the York Police.

He had the girl examined by medical professionals, and they confirmed that she showed the unmistakable signs of having recently given birth. At this point she broke down and confessed that the baby was buried in her parents' garden.

28 APRIL 1489 Nothing is guaranteed to incense the population like a new and seemingly unjust tax. Henry VII wanted to send military aid to Brittany to help it retain independence from France, but to do so he had to raise £100,000 in taxation, and part of that burden fell on Yorkshire. However, the previous year the crops had failed, and many felt that they shouldn't have to go through hard times to help people they had no connection with whatsoever. Henry Percy, 4th Earl of Northumberland, was despatched from York to plead with the king, but came back empty handed. As he approached the city he was met by a band of rebels led by his illegitimate cousin, Sir John Egremont. When he gave them the bad news, it is safe to say that they didn't take it well. In fact he was dragged from his horse and lynched at the side of the road.

29 APRIL 1942 Following the bombing of Lübeck in Germany, Adolf Hitler ordered a series of bombing raids on historic cities in Britain. These later became known as the Baedeker Blitz, because the targets were allegedly chosen from a Baedeker guidebook from cities awarded three stars or above. On this date, York was bombed in one of these raids and suffered heavy damage. Ninety-two people were killed and many hundreds injured. The Guildhall and the church of St Martin-le-Grand were completely gutted and other buildings, including the Rowntree's factory and the railway station, were severely damaged.

St Martin-le-Grand church in Coney Street, after the Baedeker air raid. (Author's collection)

30 APRIL 1666 A group of young men from Birdsall in the East Riding travelled to Eddlethorpe Woods, near to Castle Howard, to select and cut down a good yew tree in order to make a maypole for their Mayday celebrations the next day. In the darkness of the wood, a gun was heard to go off and one of the party, by the name of William Knaggs, cried out and then fell to the ground dead. Shortly afterwards a man named Edward Ruddock came charging out of the woods waving a gun and a pitchfork and shouting at the men, calling them rogues and saying, 'It is more fit that you were in your beds than here at this time of night!' When he was told that Knaggs was dead, he replied that he would make an example for all the rest and went away. Ruddock was later arrested but acquitted because none of the witnesses could testify to having seen him actually fire the gun.

MAY

A modern version of the famous *Flying Scotsman*.

1 MAY

1598 On this date, two men were travelling together to York when they were apprehended on information given to the authorities. One was Father Peter Snow, who had left his home in Ripon some years earlier after coming under suspicion of failing to conform to the established Church. He had since been ordained into the Catholic priesthood, and was travelling with Ralph Grimston, a Catholic layman from the village of Nidd. Both men were tried and found guilty under various acts of Catholic repression and executed at York on 15 June. Their severed heads were later displayed on spikes in the town. Nearly 250 years later, in 1845, some excavations in Hazlewood Castle near Tadcaster turned up a pair of skulls, which were initially taken to be those of the Catholic martyrs John Lockwood and Edmund Catherick. However, it was later suggested that they were Snow and Grimston, and scientific investigation has shown that this is almost certainly the correct identification. Reconstruction work on the skulls has since provided images of the faces of the two men, and the skulls are now held as relics within the altar of Leeds Cathedral.

2 MAY

1903 Mary Ann Barker was a woman said to have been of dissolute habits, and on this afternoon she was found drunk in the street by a neighbour and taken home and put to bed. Her husband John, a soldier who had returned from active duty in Malta a few weeks earlier, was soon seen to enter the house, and later appeared in the doorway with his shirt sleeves rolled up and his hands and arms covered in blood. He informed their next-door neighbour, Mrs Barnard, that if she wanted to say goodbye to his wife, she should go upstairs. The woman did and found Mrs Barker lying on the bed with her throat cut and a razor lying next to her. Barker immediately confessed to the crime and gave himself up to the police. It seemed that while he was away, he had been regularly sending money home to his wife; she, meanwhile, had been carrying on an affair with a man named Tom Childs. Barker had found out about the affair and threatened to leave Mary Ann, whereupon she agreed to give the other man up, but the next day he learned that she had spent the previous night with him. When Barker challenged her, she screamed that Childs was a better man than he, and picked up the razor, threatening to cut him. He disarmed her, and in a rage carried out the deed. The court took pity on him and found him guilty of manslaughter rather than murder, so that he was spared the noose and instead served a five-year prison sentence. A sequel to this story has already appeared in the entry for 20 April.

3 MAY

1800 When asked at his trial at York Castle if he pleaded guilty or not guilty, Granville Medhurst responded, 'Is there a Saviour on Earth, eh?' This was simply the latest in a series of bizarre actions which began when, at around 8 p.m. on this evening, he sent his servant Thomas Spinke home, telling him he wished his family to go to bed. On Spinke's return at 6.30 the following morning, the servant was met by two of the children of the house, clearly upset, who led him to their parents' bedroom. There he saw Mrs Medhurst clearly dead on the bed. Immediately Spinke's employer emerged from behind the curtains covered in blood and, brandishing a sword, ordered him to leave the room and then locked the door. Spinke took the children to a nearby public house, and returned with a group of neighbours who attempted to gain entry to the house but could not. Mr Greene, the magistrate, arrived and ordered Medhurst to throw his weapons from the window, but the man replied that he would not give up his house. Later, Medhurst called for Spinke to bring him his boots so that he could die like a man. While Greene distracted him, a man named Longbotham managed to climb in through a rear window, pick the lock of the room, and surprise Medhurst from behind. Spinke testified in court that his employer had been behaving strangely for some time, and had expressed a concern that his wife was going to murder him so she could marry another man. Mrs Medhurst was found to have twelve stab wounds made with the sword. Granville was found not guilty due to insanity, and sent to an asylum for life.

4 MAY 1876 Alexander McTurk was the guard on the *Flying Scotsman*. His son 22-year-old son Robert, said to be a 'great strong young fellow', was an idle layabout. His father had found him a series of employments but he had refused to attend any one, and also refused to leave his father's house in St Paul's Terrace, spending all of the man's money and threatening him with violence when he objected. After causing serious damage to the front door and stating that he would stab his father and set the house on fire, Alexander was finally persuaded to take his son to court on this date. The bench committed him to fourteen days' imprisonment and bound him over to keep the peace. When asked if he agreed to be bound over, he replied that he did not, and consequently his prison sentence was increased to six months.

5 MAY 1908 An inquest was held into the death of Margaret Eleanor Brown, a governess who had apparently died whilst undergoing an illegal abortion performed by a Dr Gramshaw of Bootham, who operated out of a surgery in Low Ousegate. Her death had been as a result of acute peritonitis. On 4 May the inquest had heard the testimony of Dr Gramshaw's assistant, and some question came up as to whether or not he had had the correct equipment to carry out such a surgery, and if he did not, whether he had hastened her death. Dr Gramshaw himself attended, but was said to be withdrawn and looking as if he did not quite comprehend. The following day, he was due to give evidence himself, but did not turn up at the inquest. On enquiry, he was found in a

comatose state in his bed, and had apparently injected himself with a combination of laudanum and morphia. Although doctors attending him were able to bring him back to consciousness for brief periods, he never fully recovered and died two days later.

6 MAY 1817 Following a day of races at the Knavesmire, a family by the name of Barwick were returning home and crossing the carriage road leading away from the racecourse on foot. Major General Sir John Byng, a military hero of some note, had just left the races in his carriage, and Barwick's daughter, who was carrying her 11-month-old child in her arms, was tending to the child and did not notice the carriage, straying too close. As she did so, she was clipped by one of the horses and fell, releasing the baby, which rolled underneath the carriage and was crushed under the wheels. The girl herself was also badly injured in the accident. An inquest found that nobody was to blame, and that the coach driver had done everything possible to try to avoid the accident.

7 MAY 1913 Holgate Beck is a stream that runs between the main railway lines leading into York station and a busy residential area. Although on private property, it was easily accessed from the residential side and the children regularly played beside it. It is quite deep at several points, however, and according to Albert Watson, who lived in Stamford Street, a child falling in had become almost a weekly occurrence. Nonetheless, nothing had been done about securing access, and on this date Mr Watson's 7-year-old son Sidney was poking around in the water with a stick when he overbalanced and disappeared into the water. Herbert Clark, who lived at the end of the road, saw the incident and ran to recover the child, but although he fished him out of the water quickly, he was unable to revive him and Sidney was pronounced dead shortly afterwards.

8 MAY 1896 Albert Fisher, a 31-year-old shunter at York railway station, was found unconscious on the pavement in Railway Street early in the morning and rushed to hospital, where he died a week later. Death was due to an inflammation of the membrane of the brain caused by a fractured skull, and this evidently occurred when the man hit his head on the pavement after a fall. He had been in company with other men the previous evening (this date) and one of them, named Richardson, had been accused of pushing him, causing the fall. The medical examiner was of the opinion that there was no evidence of this having happened, and the man himself denied it. Summing up at the inquest into the death, the coroner suggested that the various discrepancies in the evidence of the case were due to the fact that almost everybody who had given that evidence had been too drunk at the time to actually remember anything at all.

9 MAY 1825 Following the York races on this day, a number of soldiers from the 6th Inniskilling Dragoons stationed in the city were in one of the refreshment tents and one of the soldiers was talking to a local man named William Marshall, who mentioned that he had seen more service, having been a serving soldier for sixteen years. The other man took offence at this and struck Marshall in the face. Marshall fought back and others came to his aid, whereupon the man's fellow soldiers also joined in the fight. Within moments a full-scale riot had ensued, with the soldiers taking up the tops of trestle tables to use as weapons, and the fight soon spilled out of the tent and on to the racetrack. At its height, upward of 100 people are said to have been involved and, with the locals having far greater numbers, the soldiers turned and ran for the river, towards the Fulford ferry. However, there were too many for the capacity of the boat, and as they all attempted to get on board, it capsized and spilled them out into the river. At this point, many of the locals forgot their anger and helped the men to shore.

10 MAY 1859 At the December assizes in York in 1858, two cases had come before the court of young men who had murdered their paramours in a fit of passion while believing them to be taking up with another man. John Whitworth was sentenced to death, while James Atkinson was found not guilty on the grounds of insanity. At Whitworth's execution, there was a near riot and cries from the crowd that Atkinson's crime had been by far the worse and that he should be next to Whitworth on the gallows. Much of Atkinson's insanity plea had been based around attempts he had made in the prison to hang himself. Atkinson was placed in York Castle, where his behaviour was erratic and included several suicide attempts and physical attacks on guards and the governor himself, leading to him eventually being taken to St George's asylum. However, on this date Thomas Dove, who had shared a cell with Atkinson, shed some light on the matter, testifying that Atkinson had shared with him plans to get taken to the asylum where he considered he could live out his sentence in relative luxury compared to the hard labour he had received at the castle. According to Dove, Atkinson had explained to him exactly where and when his next suicide attempt would take place, entreating him to act shocked and cut him down, and giving him a suicide note which he asked him to give to the governor after his 'rescue'. The affair caused something of a scandal, causing the British Medical Association to tighten up their procedures regarding insanity pleas.

11 MAY 1537 At the time of the Reformation, Carthusian monks were held in higher esteem in the country than almost all other orders, due to their secluded and peaceful nature and the sincerity of their mode of life. As such, Henry VIII courted the favour of the order in his scheme to take personal control of the Church, but was rejected

in this endeavour. As a result, he set about the systematic destruction of the London Charterhouse of the Carthusians, and several were sentenced to death on charges of treason and hanged at the Tyburn in London. Others were seized, and two, John Rochester and James Walworth, were sent to Hull and detained there. Following the Pilgrimage of Grace there were mutterings in York of a further uprising by the Catholic faithful, and it was decided that a public spectacle might discourage such action. The two monks were sent for and brought to the city, where they were tried on charges of treason by the High President of the Council of the North, with great ceremony. Sentenced to death, they were hung in chains from the city battlements, with instructions that their bodies were to remain hanging until they fell to pieces.

12 MAY 1901 Frederick Hawtin, Thomas Robson and James Richardson had been drinking for most of the day when, in the late afternoon, they decided to hire a rowing boat and go out for a trip on the River Ouse. Richardson, a sailor on HMS *Mermaid*, took the oars, and the other two sat in the stern. No sooner were they away from shore than the men started larking around in their inebriated state, and as a result the boat turned over and all were thrown into the river. Robson, knowing that Hawtin was unable to swim, tried to get him to a nearby boat and asked for them to put out an oar to bring them on board, but the owners refused, saying, 'you'll swamp us too'. There were several other boats on the river, but all had seen the way the men were behaving and were similarly concerned that letting them on board would spell disaster for themselves. Eventually, Hawtin became so panicked that Robson feared for his own life if he kept trying to rescue the man, so left him to his fate. Hawtin was drowned, although the other two made it safely out of the water.

13 MAY 1816 William Nadin worked in the city as a well sinker. A dangerous line of work at the best of times, this regularly involved working underground in dank conditions. On this date, as he was around 7ft below the surface in Smedley Lane in the city, the ground above him collapsed. His son, who was working with him at the time, managed to scramble clear, but Nadin was buried underneath the cave-in. By the time rescue workers were able to dig him out, it was too late, and Nadin had suffocated to death.

14 MAY 1912 J.P. Wood, the longstanding coroner for York, stated at the end of an enquiry held on this date that it had been a painful duty to have to conduct this inquest into the death of his friend Walter Llewellyn Fry, who held the equivalent position for Catterick. Fry had been found dead the day before at York railway station. He had recently checked himself into a retreat in York, complaining of overwork, and his mental condition had since been said to be improving although he still suffered long bouts of depression. The day before he had been visited by his wife and a friend named Henry Seeker and he had gone to the station to see them off on their trains, seemingly in good cheer at the time. However, he was found around an hour later in the toilet at the station, where he had used a razor to slash a 2in-deep cut in his left groin, which had severed the femoral artery and resulted in his bleeding to death.

15 MAY 1866 A young girl named Sarah Kilvington, from a respectable family who lived near Malton, entered service in York with the Smith family of Marygate, where she took up the role of housemaid and shared a bed each night with fellow servant Margaret Stapylton. Members of the household had noticed that the girl was growing larger and suspected a pregnancy, but Kilvington denied this and as she had always acted with the utmost propriety, the family were inclined to believe her. However, on the Saturday night before this date the pair went to bed, and at 3 a.m. Stapylton was awoken by her bedmate, who was in great pain. She left to fetch some gin and water to ease the pain, and left the girl in her room while she went about her morning's work. On her return she found the room in disarray and blood on the sheets. A doctor was called for who, after examining the girl and becoming convinced that she had recently delivered a child, discovered a box containing the body of a newborn girl. At the inquest, held on this day, he described finding an apron string around the baby's neck, and stated that the child had been born alive and then strangled. The girl later claimed that she had used the apron string to help her deliver the child and that it had died shortly afterwards. At her trial the jury gave her the benefit of the doubt, but she was found guilty of concealment of the birth and sentenced to one year's hard labour.

16 MAY 1528 Although Henry VIII would shortly embrace the Protestant Church, at this point England was still a Catholic country and strongly resisted the tide of Protestantism spreading across Northern Europe. On this date, a punishment was handed down to a Dutchman by the name of Gilbert Johnson or Johannes residing in York, after he had testified that he would make confession only to God and not to any priest, pope or archbishop. His punishment was to precede the cross on a procession from York Minster to St Mary's Abbey clad only in his shirt, and was to submit to the discipline of the Dean of the Minster at various points along the way. The following day he was to repeat the process in the suburbs of York, again on the Saturday of the week in the Pavement, where he was to be disciplined in each corner of the market, and finally on the Sunday, in his

own parish of Coneygarth. Although this punishment does not sound harsh, undoubtedly crowds would have lined the route on each occasion to pelt him with stones and rotting fruit and vegetables, and to make the experience as unpleasant as possible.

17 MAY 1909 Private Thomas Brannigan came up before the York police court on this morning after his drunken behaviour the previous Saturday night had caused a riot to take place in the city. Brannigan was said to have attempted to climb one of the parapets of the Ouse Bridge when a military policeman, Lance Sergeant Clemshaw, attempted to stop him. Brannigan began to beat the man with a stick, and when Clemshaw's colleague, Private Samuel Purt, tried to aid the officer, Brannigan began to beat and kick him as well. As the two men tried to get him under control, a man named Gowen Stoker joined in, dragging Clemshaw off of the man. By now several other people had started to take notice and joined in the affray. At its height, between 400 and 500 people were said to have been involved, and five policemen and six military policemen were hurt in the rioting that ensued. Brannigan was given a month's hard labour as punishment.

18 MAY 1904 Arthur Bell, a cycle agent living in Micklegate, was asked by a Mrs Reed, an acquaintance in the village of Escrick, to take in as a lodger a girl named Dora Turnbull who had been staying at her house. Turnbull arrived on Monday 15th, and the next day complained of feeling unwell. By the Wednesday she seemed to be herself again, but that evening Bell's wife confided in him her suspicion that the girl had been pregnant and given birth to a child. On this date, Bell went to the police station and returned with a Detective Whittaker, who searched her property and found a box containing the body of a newborn child. The child appeared to be unmarked, but doctors inspecting it stated that it had been born alive and had died due to inattention at birth. Whittaker then travelled to Escrick to search possessions Turnbull had left there, and in a hatbox he found the remains of another child, this one evidently dead for over a year. It transpired that the girl, originally from near Newcastle, had carried three previous children, all of whom had also died very shortly after birth.

19 MAY 182 At 2 a.m., Simon Hargreaves, together with Rufus Sunderland and William Bremer, attempted to sell some goods to a man named Garforth in Hunslet Lane. The goods had been stolen from a man named William Scott a few hours previously, and the three men were apprehended soon after the attempted transaction and taken to York Castle. On his arrest, Hargreaves is said to have had a stolen boiled egg in his pocket. The rest of the stolen goods were also foodstuffs. For this, the three men were sentenced to death, although their sentences were later commuted to transportation overseas for life. Sent to

Melbourne in Australia, Hargreaves is said to have attempted to escape three times before finally settling down to life there, later becoming a successful businessman. His story is featured prominently today in the York Castle Museum.

20 MAY 1840 Eleven years after Jonathan Martin's arson attack, York Minster was in flames again on this night. The fire was said to have been started by a spark from a lamp taken in by a workman mending a clock in the south-west tower. An eyewitness account stated, 'The shouting of the firemen, the roaring of the flames rushing up the tower with the rapidity of a furnace draught, sounded in the high and arched spaces awful and terrific. The falling masses of wood and bells sounded like the near discharge of artillery, and were echoed back from the dark passages, whose gloomy shades and hollow responses seemed mourning at the funeral pyre that burned so fiercely. In one hour the tower was completely gutted, and masses of burning timber lay piled against the south-west door.'

21 MAY 1108 The death of Gerard, Archbishop of York, did not take place in or near the city; in fact, he was travelling to London at the time. How he died is not known. His body was found at the side of a road, in an orchard, and close to him was a copy of a book of 'curious arts', most likely Julius Fermicus Maternus's book *Ancient Astrology*. This, along with his ownership of a Hebrew psalter and his encouragement of one of his clergy to study Hebrew, led to rumours of his being involved in sorcery. William of Malmesbury, the medieval historian, accused Gerard of 'immorality, avarice and the practice of magic', and described him as 'lewd and lustful'. After his death his remains were returned to York, but because of his reputation, and his attempts to force reforms on his clergy and chapter against their will, he was refused burial in the minster, and was instead buried outside near the porch. His successor, Thomas, had his remains exhumed and moved inside.

22 MAY 1891 Harry Hewitt, a militiaman from Sheffield, entered a lodging house in Hungate on this day and was said to have been behaving so strangely that one of the residents of the house, a Mrs Rawson, rushed next door to fetch her neighbour's husband to deal with the incident. When Thomas Coates returned with her, they found the door locked, and Hewitt standing in an upstairs window holding a knife to his own throat. Shouting 'I'll do it, I'll do it', he began to cut into his own flesh, so Coates broke the door down and rushed to the upstairs room, where Hewitt rushed at him with the knife, shouting, 'First come, first served!' Coates managed to block the knife with a wooden hairbrush he picked up from the nightstand, and disarmed the other man, who was found to be bleeding profusely from the self-inflicted neck wound.

23 MAY 1864 On this date, a young man named Thomas Palfreyman died in the hospital in York, two days after being stabbed in a bar fight. The fight had taken place in the Queen's Head public house in Fossgate. Palfreyman and some others had gone into the kitchen of the establishment and found a group of Irishmen drinking in there. Details of exactly what happened are sketchy, but some kind of quarrel arose between the two groups, which turned into a scuffle, and in the middle of this Palfreyman is said to have cried out, 'I'm stabbed! I'm stabbed!' At this point, a surgeon was called and found that the young man had been sliced open to a length of 6–8in with his intestines protruding through the wound. Another wound was found in his right-hand side, and the following day Palfreyman was able to give a statement from his hospital bed that the perpetrator was one of the Irishmen, a labourer named John Foy. At his trial he was found guilty of manslaughter, but because he had originally claimed that another of his party was responsible, and named that man, the judge gave him the maximum sentence for the crime, which was twenty years' penal servitude.

24 MAY 1888 Charlotte Hampshire, a 63-year-old woman from West Cottingwith, arose this morning as she usually did, prepared her son's breakfast and packed him off to work in her usual cheerful manner, then cleared up the kitchen and hanged herself from a rafter by a piece of cord. She was found by one of her two daughters who also lived in the house; the girl ran outside and found the village postman, William Wood, who cut her down and tried to revive her, but to no avail. No explanation was ever discovered as to why she would want to take her own life.

25 MAY 1537 John Pickering was a native of Yorkshire who entered the Dominican order, and later studied to become a Doctor of Theology at Cambridge University. He was appointed Prior of the Dominican order in York and attended the Northern Convocation, which acknowledged Henry VIII as the head of the Church in England, although he violently opposed this measure. As a result he became involved in the Pilgrimage of Grace, the armed uprising in the North against the Dissolution of the Monasteries. One of his most notable contributions was the writing of a 150-line poem calling people to arms against southern heretics, which was set to music and became a battle hymn of the uprising. He later became involved in Bigod's Rebellion, a second uprising protesting Henry's failure to act on his promises after the pilgrimage, and it was as a result of this that he was arrested and singled out for a special prosecution. Found guilty of high treason, he was hanged, drawn and quartered on this date. The fate of his remains is unknown.

26   MAY 1858   An inquest was held into the death of Charles Rotherforth, a 16-year-old boy who had been in service with Mr William Frankish, a farmer in Dunnington. Several weeks before on a Saturday, although nobody was quite sure of the date, Mr Frankish had intended to head to market in York when he found that his boots had not been cleaned. He sent his female servant, Sarah Barker, to instruct Rotherforth to do so, and she returned, saying that he had refused. Frankish and Barker then went to see the boy, who claimed he had not refused, but Barker was adamant he had. Frankish had had some drink at the time and became enraged, kicking the boy in the back. Since that time he had complained regularly of back pain, and around two weeks before this date he returned to his parents' house barely able to move. On the Saturday doctors were called and found him in a rigid condition and in a great deal of pain. He was diagnosed with tetanus, probably caused by the kick, and although taken to the hospital where every effort was made to save him, he died a few days later.

27   MAY 1872   An inquest held on this date heard the details of a bizarre accident that occurred at the Rowntree's chocolate factory in Tanner's Moat. Isaac Dickenson, in charge of one of the boilers, was in a hurry to get home from his day's shift and – in order to cool the engine off more quickly – chose to unscrew the iron manhole cover on the top of the main drum. Unfortunately, the pressure build-up inside caused this lid to come away with a force that actually lifted him to the ceiling of the building, which he struck before falling again to the ground. By the time others reached him, they found that he had sustained a dreadful head injury in the fall and was severely scalded from the steam from the boiler. He survived for less than half an hour.

28   MAY 1787   According to legend, Kitty Garthwaite was a pretty young girl from the village of Gillamoor who was engaged to Willie Dixon of nearby Hutton-le-Hole. The pair had been intimate, and Garthwaite fell pregnant. She informed her lover of her condition as they picnicked near a brook and the pair fell into an argument which resulted in Dixon riding away on his horse, abandoning the young girl. He had not gone far when he had a change of heart and instead of heading home, set off for York to obtain a marriage license. Sadly, it would never be used as the following morning, on this date, Kitty's body was found drowned in the brook, clad in only a white sark or undershirt. The next day, Dixon drowned in the same place, said to have been lured there by an apparition of Kitty sitting naked by the water's edge. Over the next twenty years, a further sixteen men met the same fate at the hands of the ghost known as Sarkless Kitty until in 1809, when the spirit is said to have been exorcised.

29 MAY 1661 During the English Civil War, York had remained loyal to the king, and rejoiced greatly at the reinstatement of the monarchy in the form of his son, Charles II. This date being the new king's birthday, the people decided to celebrate this fact by executing Oliver Cromwell for his role in the death of Charles' father, notwithstanding the fact that the man himself had been dead for some three years. Accordingly, they created an effigy of the former Lord Protector and dressed him in a pink satin suit. They set up a gallows outside the church of All Saints, Pavement, and hanged the effigy with great ceremony before placing it inside a tar barrel to be burned. Over 1,000 citizens of York are said to have turned out to witness the execution.

30 MAY 1323 The Great Council of the North was held at Bishopthorpe on this date, to make a treaty and end the ongoing conflicts with the Scots. Over the previous two decades, Edward II had led several armies north of the border to try and complete the conquest of Scotland begun by his father. In May 1322, a two-year truce expired and Edward, who had moved his government to York earlier that year, spent that summer planning another campaign, which would turn out to be something of a disaster. With an army estimated around 30,000 men, he crossed the border on 10 August, but had spent so long in preparation that Robert the Bruce was ready for the invasion and had had all crops and livestock removed along the way, taking his own army to the isles. The result was that by the time Edward reached Edinburgh, his supplies were running dry and he had no choice but to retreat. At this point, the Scots returned and continually attacked the now demoralised and poorly supplied army all the way back to England. Later that year, Bruce attacked York in retaliation (see 14 October), and while his army did not enter the city, they reached the gates and set fire to the suburbs, leaving Edward with no choice but to sue for peace.

31 MAY 1591 Thomas Watkinson was a widower who lived a solitary life in a small cottage in the village of Menthorpe, in the East Riding. Although he made no secret of being a Catholic to his friends and neighbours, he was also careful never to openly flout the laws against Catholicism. However, on the night before Palm Sunday of 1591, he was spotted gathering palms close to his property, and there was a suspicion that this would be in order to hold a religious service. This was reported to the local magistrate, who raided his home the following morning and found a Catholic priest, Robert Thorpe, preparing to conduct the service. The two men were arrested and sent to London, where they were tortured by the notorious 'priest hunter' Richard Topcliffe, who demanded they named others involved in their circle. Both men, however, refused to break. Eventually they were returned to York where, on this date, Thorpe was hanged, drawn and quartered as a traitor, while Watkinson was merely hanged, the punishment for the harbouring of priests.

JUNE

King Richard III. (Author's collection)

1 JUNE 1835 An innocent wrestling match ended in death on this date in the village of Helmsley, just north of York. John Sigsworth, a chaise driver, and George Bland, a shoemaker, were friends who often spent time together in the village. On this occasion, Bland was passing the stable where Sigsworth was employed and suggested that the men wrestle to see who was the strongest. The affair was not fractious, but intended merely as sport; however, during the course of the contest, Sigsworth dropped Bland on his head, and it was as a result of this that the latter man died. Sigsworth was charged with manslaughter, but a jury agreed that the death was accidental and he was acquitted.

2 JUNE 1810 Matthew Agar, a 25-year-old from York, was convicted at the Lent Assizes for the theft of a chestnut mare, and was now under sentence of death. The deputy gaoler at York Castle, Samuel Wilson, became suspicious on this date after Agar had received a visit from his younger brother John, and as a consequence he examined the prisoner's leg irons and found them nearly sawn through. A search of the area turned up a small saw in the privy. As a result, John Agar was arrested and joined his brother in the castle until the following assizes, where he was tried. Evidence was introduced to the court that the younger man had purchased a saw similar to the one found, while his only defence was a string of character witnesses testifying that he was an honest man. This, apparently, was good enough for the jury, who found him not guilty. Matthew, meanwhile, escaped the noose when his sentence was commuted to transportation for life.

3 JUNE 1832 On this date, a surgeon at York Dispensary was summoned to Skeldergate to attend one Thomas Hughes, a 21-year-old waterman who was suffering from a 'severe purging and vomiting and afflicted by violent spasms at the stomach'. Within two days it had been confirmed that the cholera epidemic spreading through the country had reached York. Hughes lived in a rather filthy courtyard known locally as the Hagworm's Nest, and from here the disease began to spread across the city, particularly in the more unsanitary districts. By the time the disease had run its course in October of that year, 450 cases had been diagnosed and 185 deaths reported.

4 JUNE 1516 A meeting of the Royal Council was held on this day to give judgement on a matter that had been plaguing the town since February. On the first of that month, an election had been held for a new alderman for the city, and the two leading candidates, John Norman and William Cure, had received exactly the same

number of votes. As a result, the citizens began to side with one candidate or another, and fighting broke out on the streets between the two factions. This continued until 6 April, when the leading aldermen were summoned to appear before Thomas Wolsey, who passed the matter into the council's hands. Their judgement, on this date, was that neither man should be elected, and that the seat should remain empty. The following year another alderman died, and it was decided that both men should now be given one of the vacant places.

5 JUNE 1871 Matthew Cook was a watchmaker who kept a shop in Goodramgate, and was said to be a man of intemperate habits who suffered from delerium tremens. On this date he, his wife Sarah and their youngest child, just 18 months of age, had been walking near Haxby Road and Cook had apparently asked his wife for money for drink, which she had denied him. Flying into a rage, he took the child from her and flung it aside, before attacking her and stabbing her twice in the throat; she later died as a result of her wounds. He then attempted to cut his own throat and when another man named Demney – alerted by the cries of the child – arrived at the scene, Cook screamed at him to fetch him a bigger knife so he could finish the job. At his trial he was found to be not guilty by reason of insanity, and was remanded to an asylum for life.

6 JUNE 1932 While boating on the River Derwent near Stamford Bridge, a party of three men and two young boys from York failed to notice a large waterfall and became caught in its influence. As the boat neared the edge, George Long managed to leap from the boat and get ashore, but the other four occupants went over and were thrown into the water below. Walter Herbert, the father of the two boys, managed to cling to his youngest son Harry, who was just 4 years old, and got him to safety. His other son, Walter, was nowhere to be seen, but the other man, Walter Bardy, dived repeatedly until he found him and dragged him to the shore, where they managed to revive him. Miraculously nobody was seriously hurt, unlike thirty years earlier, when three men had been killed going over the same waterfall.

7 JUNE 1888 William Brownley Megginson was a reporter for the *Yorkshire Weekly Gazette* and had been away on holiday with his family at Scarborough until this week when he had returned home on the Tuesday evening. During his vacation, Megginson had complained of dizziness and light-headedness, but set off for his place of work on the Wednesday morning in good cheer. He never arrived. On this date his body was discovered floating in the River Ouse near to Naburn Lock. It was the verdict of his inquest that it was impossible to know how he came to be there.

8 JUNE 1405 After successfully deposing Richard II in 1399, Henry Bolingbroke was escorted to the vacant throne by his two archbishops, Thomas Arundel of Canterbury, and Richard le Scrope of York. However, things did not go well for the new king; his claims on the French throne were rejected and the Welsh revolted against him under Owain Glyndwr. As a result of his military campaigns, Henry was forced to raise taxes, and his former allies the Percy family took up arms against him. Scrope was closely associated with the Percys, and raised an army of approximately 9,000 townspeople of York. They waited on Shipton Moor to join up with the main Percy forces, but were persuaded by Richard Neville, Earl of Westmorland, to stand down in return for their grievances being heard. However, when Henry arrived, he was in no mood to honour this agreement, and instead had Scrope and his co-conspirator Thomas Mowbray, Earl of Norfolk, sentenced to death. On this date their execution was carried out at Clementhorpe, in the shadow of York's walls. Scrope was led to his death through the streets of the city riding backwards on a mule but, refusing to bow to this insult, he requested that the axeman take five blows of the axe to remove his head, in memory of the five wounds of Christ.

Tomb of Richard le Scrope, Archbishop of York. (Author's collection)

9 JUNE 1875 Thomas Sword was passing along a footpath at Clifford Ings on this date when he saw a man asleep in the grass with a red handkerchief over his face. Returning along the same path twenty minutes later, the man was still there and had not shifted position, and Sword noticed that his hands were blue. He attempted to wake the man and found him to be dead. Sword then sought out a policeman, who found evidence on the man's body that he was connected to a Dr Husband, who then identified him as his dispenser, Joseph Howard, who had been due to go away that day to be married. It was further discovered that he was a widower with an 8-year-old daughter, so the police attended his house in the Groves. Finding no answer, they used keys found about his body to enter. Upstairs they discovered that the daughter was also dead, with flecks of froth around her mouth. The night before she had been put to bed by the mother of Howard's deceased wife, who stated that Howard had come home at 11 p.m. and had been behaving strangely. Mark Lacy, the brother of his intended bride, had arranged to meet him that morning to take him to the wedding, but he had failed to

turn up, and when he attended the house, Howard had not been dressed and had sent him away. It was found that the girl had been poisoned with prussic acid, and Howard had died of an overdose of morphia, both of which he could have easily obtained in his job. Why he had taken such a drastic course of action was never discovered.

10 JUNE 1930 In the village of Bishop Wilton, a little to the east of York, Mabel Jefferson, the 16-year-old daughter of the village policeman, had been spending much time in the company of 29-year-old Alfred Swaine, and on this day was due to leave the village to go into service in Shipton Thorpe. She left her family home as planned, and about 9 p.m., Swaine told his mother that there was a fox bothering chickens and asked her for their shotgun, which he took away with two cartridges. The following morning the pair were found beneath a tree, both shot with the gun; a shoelace was tied around the trigger, which Swaine had clearly used in order to pull the trigger on himself. It was said that Mabel's father was sending the girl into service in order to separate her from Swaine, as he felt that the age difference was too great and that his daughter was too young to know her own mind.

11 JUNE 1660 Richard Batty was the gamekeeper of Newby Park, a large country home belonging to Sir Metcalfe Robinson, the MP for York. On this night he came upon three poachers – William Inman, Charles Fish and Marmaduke Horseman – stalking deer in the park with a greyhound. He tried to apprehend them but was knocked to the ground by Inman. One of the other men was heard to encourage him, saying, 'hang him, and throw him into the pond'. Batty died from his injuries the following day and Sir Metcalfe, who was in London at the time of the incident, offered a £10 reward for the capture of each of the three culprits. The three fled the country, but Fish and Horseman were apprehended eight years later in London after being recognised by Batty's son George, who had been present on the night in question. All three had been convicted and sentenced to death in their absence, and so the two men were accordingly put to death.

12 JUNE 1487 The Battle of Stoke Field on 16 June is regarded as the final battle of the Wars of the Roses. Fought between King Henry VII, two years after his defeat of Richard III, and John de la Pole, Earl of Lincoln, in support of the 10-year-old Yorkist pretender Lambert Simnel, it resulted in victory for the king and effectively put an end to any hope of a York revival. The uprising had been planned in Dublin and an army of mostly Irish mercenaries arrived in Lancashire on 4 June. As they marched east across the Pennines they gathered support, most notably from the Scrope

brothers John and Thomas. As they passed York, Lord Clifford, who had command of the city, attempted to cut them off with 400 men near Tadcaster, but his force was heavily defeated and had to retreat into the city, where the Earl of Northumberland arrived with the Northern Army of 6,000 men. On this date, thinking that the rebel army had passed, Northumberland led his and Clifford's men out of the city, intent

Bootham Bar, early twentieth century. (Author's collection)

on joining Henry's main army. In order to prevent them doing so, the Scrope brothers rode for York and mounted an attack on the Bootham Bar, succeeding in capturing the barbican and demanding Simnel be crowned king. Riders were sent out of the city to alert Northumberland to return, and the Lord Mayor raised a force strong enough to keep the attacking army occupied until they could arrive. As soon as they did, the rebels retreated and set off to join their main force, content in the knowledge that Northumberland would not dare leave the city again until he was certain the danger had passed.

13 JUNE 1864 Several newspapers reported on an incident in which Mr Dykes, a locum doctor working in Davygate, was called to the home of a Miss Peckitt, a maiden lady of 90 years whose father had been a famous maker of stained-glass windows, still on display today in churches around the city, including the minster. The house, between King's Staithe and the New Walk, was found to be in a disgraceful state, filthy and with rabbits running wild inside. Miss Peckitt lived with a brother and two sisters by the name of Marshall and they had discouraged visitors for some years since. Dykes had been called to attend William Marshall, but found him to be dead and in an emaciated state, describing him as barely more than a skeleton. The occupants were said to have been in straitened circumstances for some time, but had refused all help with their condition. Marshall was said to have died of malnutrition, and had their circumstances not been discovered, the three women were in such a condition that they would have been likely to follow him soon afterwards.

14 JUNE 1803 Martha Chapel had been in service to Colonel Surtees for some months when, on this date, a doctor was called as she had complained of being unwell. Dr Turton afterwards confided in Annabella Wilson, the colonel's daughter, that he suspected that the girl was with child. Chapel denied this, but the next morning she was taken extremely ill once more and Miss Wilson attended her, whereupon Martha claimed that the doctor had told her that she had colic. Wilson then told Chapel what the doctor had said, and stated that if she was indeed carrying a child then her family would make sure she had every assistance. However, again she denied it. During this discussion, Wilson heard a noise from the other bed in the room, but the girl had claimed it was just her stomach making noises. Wilson fetched two other servants, and together they searched the bed and found the body of a newborn baby, with its throat cut across and its jaw torn off. Chapel was found guilty of murder and executed, but in his summing up on the case, the judge stated that he hoped that the man who had seduced her and left her in this condition would find his own divine judgement.

15 JUNE 1541 On this day, Sir John Neville of Chevet was executed at York Castle as a result of the Catholic West Riding Conspiracy earlier that year. A minor descendant of the Neville family who had played an important role in the Wars of the Roses, despite many reports to the contrary, Sir John was neither a Catholic nor involved in the conspiracy in any way. In fact, he had sat as juror in the prosecution of Catholic rebels after the Pilgrimage of Grace four years earlier. The conspiracy in question was an attempt to revive the pilgrimage through the assassination of Robert Holgate, Archbishop of York and President of the Council of the North. Sir John's crime, officially, was that, as Justice of the Peace for the West Riding, he had failed to report the conspiracy to the king in a timely manner and was accused of misprision, or the concealment of treason. Unofficially, he was unlucky to be associated with the Yorkists at a time when Henry VIII was attempting to wipe out all memory of that dynasty.

16 JUNE 1644 As the Siege of York neared its end, the Parliamentarian army succeeded in blowing up St Mary's Tower, part of the walls that surrounded what now remained of St Mary's Abbey. A regiment of foot soldiers under the command of Sergeant-Major Lawrence Crawford stormed the breach and entered into the abbey grounds, finding themselves on a bowling green. What happened next is now known

St Mary's Tower, rebuilt after being blown up by Parliamentarian soldiers in 1644. (Author's collection)

The bowling green on which Royalist and Parliamentarian forces clashed during the Siege of York. (Author's collection)

as the Battle of the Bowling Green, although to call it a battle is to exaggerate the event. It was closer to being a skirmish or brawl, in which the Roundhead army were repelled very quickly by Royalist forces, suffering heavy casualties in the process. Although the breach remained open, no further attempt was made on it before the siege was ended.

17 JUNE 1890 Matthew Burns was charged at York Assizes with having, on this date, had carnal knowledge of Betsy Roberts, a young girl from Clifton in York, while she was below the age of consent. Burns in his defence claimed that everything was done with consent not only of the girl, but also of the girl's parents, and that they had told him that she was 17 years of age. The girl's sister later testified that she had told Burns the year before that her sister was 15, although it turned out she had only been 14. The judge therefore ruled that on the date in question Burns had every right to believe that the girl was over 16, and that he had to dismiss the case. The fact that Burns had admitted to previous sexual congress with the girl during a time he would technically have known her to be underage was deemed inadmissible as there was no proof it occurred within the jurisdiction of the York court. In his summing up, the judge pointed out that he was only able to rule on whether the defendant had done something illegal; he was quite certain that what he had done was immoral.

18 JUNE 1914 On this afternoon a fierce thunderstorm was experienced in York. A fruiterer named Barley was making deliveries in Heslington road and had left his horse and cart in the street when a very large crash of thunder and flash of lightning frightened the horse and caused it to bolt. As the horse turned the corner, the cart was thrown into the front of the Woolpack Inn on Fawcett Street, where two men were busy painting the exterior. Both men were severely injured, and one of them, 69-year-old William Melbourne, died in hospital shortly afterwards.

The Woolpack Inn in Fawcett Street. (Author's collection)

19 JUNE 1848 On this morning, a labourer who milked the cow and did other odd jobs for Thomas Newlove and his mother, Betty, in the village of Warthill, arrived at the house to find the back door open and Mrs Newlove lying in the passage with a quantity of blood around her. The labourer raised the alarm and neighbours arrived, searched the area and discovered Thomas outside on the ground in a similar condition. An iron candlestick, which had been used to beat both of the victims, was found. Mrs Newlove recovered enough to say that three men had broken in the previous night and tried to rob the property. Her son managed to escape the house and the gang fled empty handed, thinking that he was about to raise the alarm. The pair were known in the area to hoard their money inside their house, and had close to £2,000 on the property at the time. Earlier that year, on 31 March, the house had been broken into and £690 stolen, and yet they seemed not to have learned their lesson from that incident. Although reported at first that Mrs Newlove had died from her injuries, this appears to have been an error as a legal case relating to Thomas Newlove's will from some years later states that he died the following year, and that she survived him by three years.

20 JUNE 1834 Medical science in the early nineteenth century was often a hit-and-miss affair, and people were as inclined to accept quack medicine as have a proper surgeon attend them. These medicines could often be found advertised in newspapers, or sold in apothecaries. One such was run by Joseph Webb, and when a young man named Richard Richardson began showing symptoms of smallpox on this date, having been feeling unwell for a week, it was to Webb that he turned. Webb prescribed him a remedy called Morrison's Pills and attended him for the next week, giving him these pills to take as often as three times a day. Webb continually insisted that Richardson's condition was improving, although others felt he was getting worse. After a week of steady decline, Richardson was in such a poor condition that a surgeon was called, but was unable to do anything and the young man died. A post-mortem examination found severe inflammation to the digestive tract, and an examination of the pills found them to be made mostly of aloe and gamboge (a bar resin), as well as other purgative substances which would have caused these inflammations. It was concluded that death was caused not by the smallpox itself, which it was believed was initially mild, but by the administration of the pills, which exacerbated the condition. Joseph Webb was convicted of manslaughter, and sentenced to six months in prison.

21 JUNE 1775 George Bulmer, an elderly man in his sixties and servant to a Mr Simpson in the Stonegate, was married to a woman over twenty years his junior, but on the morning of 20 June he informed his neighbours that she had died during

the night. He began making arrangements for a funeral, and on this date his relatives went to view the body. The woman had a scarf tied around her neck, but on closer examination they discovered that this was covering up severe black bruising and called in the local coroner, who established that the woman had been strangled. Bulmer, who had been out while this took place, returned and found out what had been discovered. He immediately attempted to cut his own throat, but was unsuccessful in taking his own life. He later confessed that he had recently taken up with another woman, and had strangled his wife in her sleep in order to clear the way for him to marry again.

22 JUNE 1840 On 20 June, Mary Metcalfe and her husband moved into a home in Acomb previously occupied by Charles Gowland and his wife Jane. On this date Mary noticed a smell coming from the coal cellar and, looking inside, noticed a bundle. When opened, the body of a child was discovered. It transpired that Jane Gowland had, two years earlier, had a child out of wedlock, which had been put into care. However, when she married, the authorities brought the child to her to look after. Her husband had already stated that he would not accept the child, and when it was handed to her, on 20 December 1839, she stated that her husband would never come back again. Later that day, Esther Skelton, a friend of Jane's, met Charles Gowland in York and they walked out to the house where Jane told them that the overseer of the workhouse had taken the child away again in consequence of her husband refusing to accept it. Skelton stayed with the Gowlands for two weeks, but stated she never saw the child in all that time. Ann Snell, who had looked after the child until it had been taken to Acomb, stated that it was in perfect health when she had seen it last. Doctors examining the body believed that death had either been from strangulation or a blow to the face, and that the body showed signs of many other serious injuries sustained before death. Jane Gowland was tried for murder, but neither she nor her husband testified, and her defence attorney suggested that the child found may not have been hers and that all evidence was purely circumstantial. The jury accordingly found her not guilty.

23 JUNE 1862 The Cooke family of St Mary, Bishophill, sat down to dinner and shortly afterwards were all taken ill with severe sickness and vomiting. Doctors were called and treated the family, who all recovered, and suspicion fell on a parsley sauce, which may have accidentally contained a poisonous ingredient. However, this was proved false, and a few days later the same occurred again, with the cook also falling ill. It was discovered that arsenic had been mixed in with the salt and flour in the kitchens. Although it was felt that this could not have happened by accident, no culprit

or motive was forthcoming and no more was thought about it until 19 November, when the same happened again. Once again, the whole family survived and this time the poison was found to have been cooked into their food. Suspicion fell on Maria Cooke, the wife of a relative of the family, who worked and lived in their shop in Coney Street. She had often complained of the family's treatment of her, and had told a servant she wanted to do something to them. The servant, Alice Clancey, claimed that Mrs Cooke had tried to bribe her into buying rat poison and putting it in the flour bin at the Bishophill home, which she said she refused to do. However, with evidence showing that Mrs Cooke had not been near the Bishophill house for some considerable time prior to both sets of events, the case against her was dropped.

24 JUNE 1882 John and Mary Devine, who lived in Heslington Road, regularly travelled into the city on a Saturday to attend the markets, and this day was no different. They were said to have quarrelled during the day, and this continued all the time they were away from their home, including a stop in the city to drink in a public house. Around midnight, Mrs Devine went to bed and fell asleep, and some time later was awoken by a pain in her throat and found that her husband was taking a knife to it. She screamed and clutched the hand holding the knife, although by now she had received a 2in wound, and in the struggle she incurred a second lengthy gash on her face. Her husband was shouting, 'I'll finish you, you bitch', and this noise brought another occupant of the house – an artilleryman named Brassey – to the room, where he managed to rescue the woman. Initially, Devine denied attacking his wife and claimed that he did not own a knife, but he later changed his story to say that he was too drunk to understand what he was doing at the time of the attack. He was sentenced to nine months in prison.

25 JUNE 1887 A report appeared in the *York Herald* of this date under the heading 'Death by Injudicious Eating'. It reported that a woman named Hannah Elizabeth Orrey, of Toft's Green, ate a plate of meat and onions at some time after 10 p.m. one night and was immediately seized with pain in her chest accompanied by vomiting; within a very short time she was dead. The coroner concluded that it was the eating of onions so late at night that had caused a spasm in the stomach and had stopped the woman's heart.

26 JUNE 1737 According to a letter published in many newspapers, a man took board and lodging at the Ferry Inn in Brough, in the East Riding of Yorkshire on this date, giving his name as John Palmer. This, however, was merely an alias to disguise the arrival of a man whose name has become synonymous with the city of

York, the notorious highwayman Richard 'Dick' Turpin. Representing himself as a horse trader, between this time and October of the following year he insinuated himself into the social life of the county, attending the best parties in York, riding with the local hunt, and carrying on a generally flamboyant lifestyle funded by his former life of highway robbery together with occasional incidents of horse theft. Turpin was on the run, having been accused of shooting Matthew King, his former partner in robbery, and having certainly shot Thomas Morris, a servant to one of the keepers of Epping Forest who had tried to arrest him.

Illustration from a 'penny dreadful' describing the adventures of Dick Turpin. (Author's collection)

27 JUNE 1816 The *York Chronicle* of this date reports on what it describes as a 'melancholy accident', which had recently occurred at the Bird in Hand Inn in the Bootham district of the city. John Sowry, described as a respectable gentleman, worked as a brewer and ostler at the establishment in question and was engaged in brewing beer. While boiling up the hops for the brew, he lost his footing and fell into the copper vat of boiling liquor. Being severely scalded across most of his body, he survived for two days in utmost agony, but eventually succumbed to infection and died. He left a wife and two young children who, having no relatives in the area, were said to have been forced to throw themselves on the goodwill of local charities with no income to sustain them.

Nineteenth-century illustration of the Bird in Hand Inn in Bootham. (Author's collection)

28 JUNE 1830 Few prisoners in York Castle have come so close to death before receiving a reprieve as William Oldfield. He was convicted at the York Assizes of having murdered his wife on this date, her body having been discovered by a lodger, William Wheatley, laying in the kitchen at the foot of a staircase with her head on the frame of a chair. Everything was covered in blood, and there were bloody footprints that appeared to lead to Oldfield's chamber door. Wheatley called out to Oldfield that his wife was dead, and he replied, 'How can I help it, the damned infernal bitch!' The doctor who was called found that she had died due to a blow to the head, but whether caused by an attack or by her falling he could not say. Oldfield stated in his defence that his wife had been drunk when he had returned home on that day, and that she had fallen out of bed twice, injuring herself and thus accounting for the bloody footprints, before leaving their bedroom. The jury, after considerable deliberation and asking additional questions to the witnesses, finally came back with a verdict of guilty, and Oldfield was sentenced to death accordingly. The execution was set for the Monday morning, and on hearing the news, Oldfield gave a cry of, 'I am a murdered man'. On the Sunday morning the surgeon involved in the case wrote to the magistrate, stating that some new evidence he had found, which meant that in his opinion, Oldfield could not possibly have been in the kitchen when the event occurred. After considering this letter for a considerable time, the magistrate signed a reprieve late on the Sunday and the man's life was spared.

29 JUNE 1811 The *York Herald* of this date reports the story of a young lad tending sheep in some marshes near the city who stopped to bathe in a body of water, went in too far and was drowned. His dog, it is stated, witnessed the events and jumped into the water to his aid. The dog managed to drag the boy to the edge of the water, and then ran to the nearby village barking loudly and alerting everyone. Some locals followed the dog back to find the unfortunate young man, but sadly they were too late to effect resuscitation.

30 JUNE 1745 The *York Courant* reported a thunderstorm on this night that caused considerable damage within the city. The report states that 'after as terrible a clap as hath been heard in the memory of man, a Pinnacle on the South East corner of the Cathedral Church, twenty-four feet high, was found split through on three sides by the Lightning, several stones of which, of a large dimension, were thrown down, one of them twelve stone weight was forced horizontally from its place near thirty yards.'

JULY

Monument marking the Marston Moor battlefield. The Royalist armies assembled in the field behind the monument, with the Parliamentarian army facing them. (Author's collection)

1 JULY 1938 With the likelihood of war approaching, the British police were preparing for possible gas attacks by setting up anti-gas schools, with one such instigated at Easingwold, north of York. On this night, several of the policemen from the school attended a dance in Oswaldkirk. Also at the dance was Gilbert Douty, a member of the wealthy Rees-Mogg family and heir to the Imperial Tobacco Company fortune. There had been some business earlier in the evening when someone had tried to take a bottle of liquor, which rested on Douty's car. When the dance was over Douty started to drive away when he heard a smashing of glass. Jumping out of the car, he began to accuse those close by of throwing a bottle, particularly one of the anti-gas school lecturers called Harry Harrison. Harrison made to strike Douty, but was restrained by his girlfriend. Meanwhile, one of the attendees of the school, Stewart Reid, a policeman from Liverpool, approached Douty, who snatched a cigarette from his mouth and threw it at him. At this point Reid struck Douty twice, after which he returned to his car, but appeared to be in distress. He was taken to York where doctors examined him and decided to send him to a nursing home. Over the next ten days his condition became progressively worse, including convulsions and frequent lapses in consciousness, and on 11 July he died. A post-mortem examination revealed a large blood clot in his brain in the area where Reid had struck him, and that his skull was abnormally thin so that the blow would likely have caused this. Reid was sent for trial for manslaughter.

2 JULY 1644 Following a major defeat at the Battle of Marston Moor during the English Civil War, survivors from the Royalist army of Prince Rupert of the Rhine made their way to York to seek refuge. Sir Henry Slingsby, who had taken part in the battle, wrote of the area around Micklegate Bar. 'We came late to York, which made a great confusion, for at the bar none were suffered to come in but such as were of the town, so that the whole street was thronged up to the bar with wounded and lame people which made a pitiful cry among them.'

3 JULY 1852 A serious disturbance occurred in Walmgate on this night, leaving many people injured and great damage to property, particularly in the area of Black Bull Lane. Shortly before midnight, a policeman named Wright was approached by a woman who asked him to go to Mrs Loy's public house, where a group of Irish patrons were refusing to leave. He identified a Michael Feeney as the ringleader and attempted to eject him, causing a fight in which Feeney was thrown across the table while four men took hold of Wright and began to beat him. Fleeing down a back alley, he was met by some more of the Irish group who began to beat him with stakes

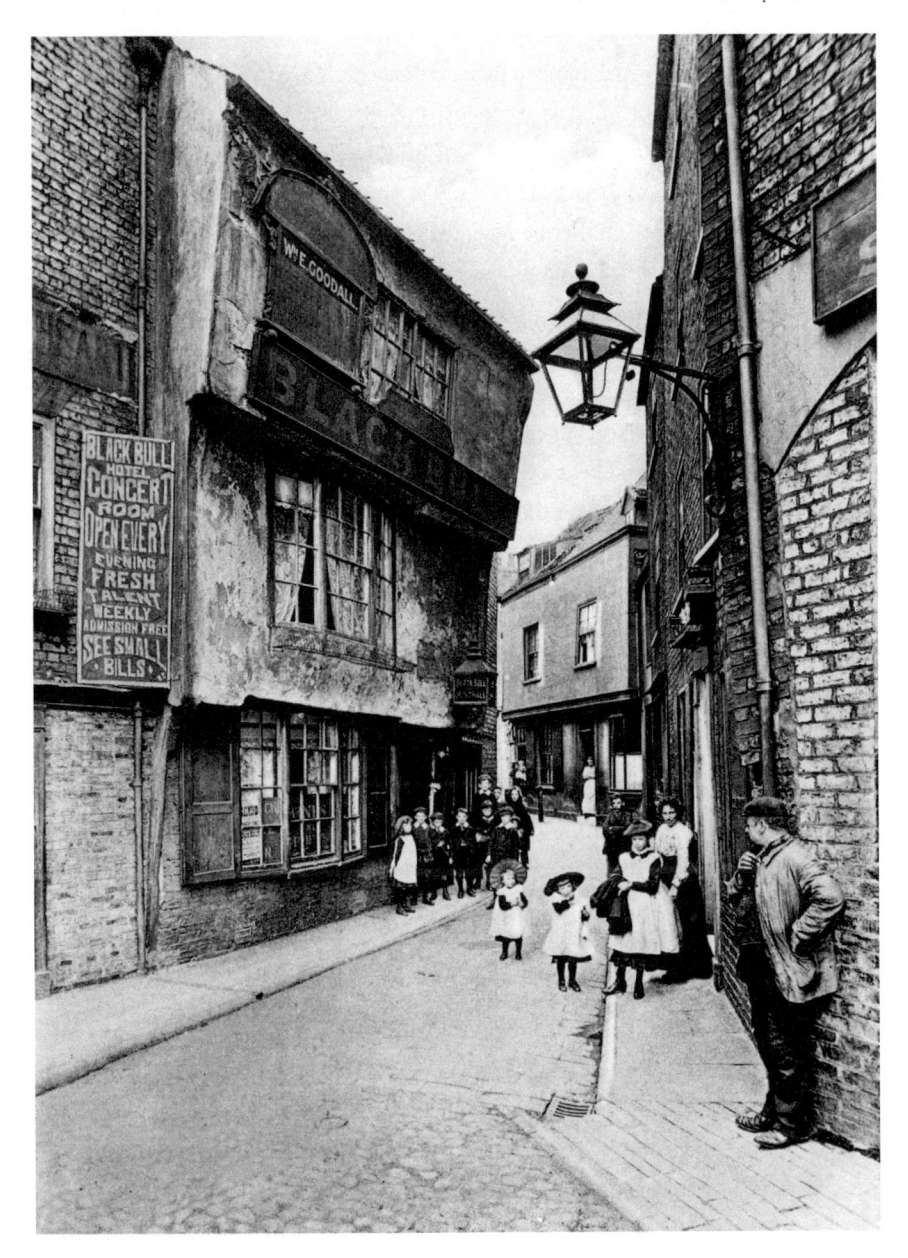

Black Bull Lane. (Author's collection)

before a group of men on the street intervened to help. By now the street scene had turned into a riot with the Irish and the newly arrived group, mostly English, fighting and throwing rocks at each other in the streets and houses in the area. Several police eventually brought things under control at around 3 a.m.

4 JULY 1597 According to Richard Challoner's *Martyrs to the Catholic Faith*, in 1596 a Protestant minister had been confined in York Castle for a misdemeanour, and in order to try to get back into the good books of his Church superiors, he befriended three Catholic priests being held there by the names of George Errington, William Knight and William Gibson, telling them that he repented of his Protestantism and wished to return to the true Catholic faith. Taking him at his word, they told him to visit one Henry Abbot after his release from the castle. Abbot promised to find a priest who could reconcile him to the faith; but he was unable to do so immediately. By now the minister had enough evidence, however, and he went to the magistrates with accusations against Abbot and the three prisoners, who were charged with crime of attempting to convert someone to the Catholic Church, which had been declared an act of treason. The three imprisoned priests were all executed in November that year. Abbot was initially reprieved, but suffered the fate of being hanged, drawn and quartered at the Knavesmire on this date.

5 JULY 1942 At around 1 a.m. in Deighton, a village south of York, a man named Henry Kirk came across Stanley Wells asleep under a tree. There was a dance breaking up nearby, and Kirk got it into his head that any girls leaving the dance and having to pass Wells would be in danger. He therefore woke Wells up and told him to leave the district, which Wells refused to do. Kirk became aggressive and Wells punched him and knocked him to the ground. Standing back up, Kirk drew a knife and stabbed Wells in the abdomen. Sentencing him to six months in prison, the judge said that he expected these things 'to happen in the Western States of America, but we don't have that sort of thing in Yorkshire'.

6 JULY 1888 The *York Herald* of this date published details of an investigation into the discovery of a body, which was found outside the Old Station in York. One of the porters at the main railway station had business in the yards of the former station, and as he walked between the two, he encountered the body lying in a shrubbery up against the city walls. The man had a revolver in his hand and a bullet wound in his forehead. The body, when found, was said to be cold and had clearly been there some time. On the body was found a note reading, 'Sick, and without friends, take care of my dear boy.' A bottle of prescription pills on the body led to the discovery that the man was William Clarke, originally of Haydon Bridge, but who had recently tried to start a grocer's business in Darlington, which had failed. He had left his son in the care of a housekeeper, saying he was going out for a walk, and had never returned.

7 JULY 1851 Elizabeth Fallan, of Water Lane, had been married for twelve years to an Irishman, Patrick Fallan, whom she had met at her home town of Sculcoates, near Kingston-on-Hull. Her husband hailed from County Sligo, and on this date she reported to the York police that shortly after their marriage, he had confided that – together with some other men – he had been in service to a Mr Percival in that county, and on finding that one of their fellow servants was a member of the Orange Order, had thrown him in some water and held his head down until he drowned. She also stated that he had fled to England after a warrant had been issued for his arrest on this crime. Patrick Fallan was arrested and put before a police court, at which his wife repeated the charge, also accusing him of bigamy. On this occasion, being clearly intoxicated while giving her testimony, and having heard that Fallan had left her recently to live with another woman, the charge was dismissed and he was released.

8 JULY 1891 An attempted suicide led to a strange scene at the York Assizes. Elizabeth Margaret Smith had been abandoned by her husband some time previously on account of her drinking, and he had got a job in Tadcaster and sent her money. However, he heard from others that she was pawning his possessions, so went to see her and found her in bed with another man while her children sat naked and dirty on a bed nearby. He then refused to give her any more money and told her that she must go to the workhouse. On this date she arranged to meet him in York and asked him to take her back, and when he refused she stood up and jumped in the river. She was brought out and revived and at the court hearing, the judge ordered that she be put in charge of her husband, who would be responsible for her future good behaviour. His response was that he would not be responsible for anything she did, at which point the judge ordered him out of court and told him he was a disgrace to his sex. He then sentenced the woman to a month in prison.

9 JULY 1984 At around 2.30 a.m., an alarm was raised that brought 150 firefighters to the site of York Minster. On the previous evening there had been a thunderstorm, and it was concluded that a lightning strike had hit a metal electrical control box attached to one of the rafters, causing a side-flash which set the rafter alight. The fire spread, and because the smoke detectors were too far down in the roof, they did not trigger until much of the roof was ablaze. The fire was contained within the south transept, and as firemen in breathing apparatus fought the blaze and attempted to prevent it reaching the central tower, staff braved the heavy smoke, burning debris and falling molten lead to rescue priceless artefacts from the area below. The fire was eventually brought under control by triggering a deliberate roof collapse, completely destroying the roof area and causing damage that eventually cost £2.25 million to repair.

Burned roof timbers in the South Transept of the minster after the fire of 1984. (Author's collection)

10 JULY 1767 On or around this date (the records are unclear), Timothy Sowerby was buried in the graveyard at Escrick, a few miles south of York. He appeared to have died of natural causes; however his wife, Ann, had since taken up with a man named John Douglas, whose wife had similarly died not long before. This caused suspicion in the public mind and eleven days later, the coroner for the city ordered an exhumation, whereupon the body was examined by an apothecary, Mr Sanderson, who detected a quantity of arsenic in the contents of the stomach. Mrs Sowerby confessed, but claimed that Douglas had first poisoned his own wife and then given her the remains of the poison. As this could not be proved, Douglas was acquitted, while Ann was burned at the stake, the standard punishment at the time for the murder of a husband by his wife.

11 JULY 1815 Mental healthcare in the nineteenth century is infamous for its mistreatment of patients. On this date, evidence was heard at an enquiry into the state of asylums in England from one Godfrey Higgins, a magistrate from the West Riding, regarding the state of York Lunatic Asylum. His testimony included the following:

> When the door was opened I went into the passage and found four cells, I think, of about 8 feet square, in a very horrid and filthy situation. The straw appeared to be almost saturated with urine and excrement, there was some bedding laid upon the straw in one cell, in the others only loose straw. A man (a keeper) was in the passage doing something, but what I do not know. The walls were daubed with excrement ... I then went upstairs, and he showed me into a room which I caused him to measure, and the size of which he told me was 12 feet by 7 feet and 10 inches, and in there were 13 women, who he told me had all come out of those cells that morning ... I became very sick, and could not remain longer in the room. I vomited.

Bootham Park Hospital, the building on the left of this photograph was formerly York Lunatic Asylum. (© Potkettle)

12 JULY 1537 The events of the Pilgrimage of Grace are described in another entry of this book for 21 October. Following the pilgrimage, Robert Aske travelled to London and was entertained by Henry VIII. While there, another noble gentleman, Thomas Bigod, began stirring up another uprising and Aske wrote to him, advising against it. Nonetheless, while Aske was on his way back to York, the uprising took place and was quickly put down. However, Henry took this as an excuse to have Aske and many other of the leaders of the previous year arrested and sent to London for trial. Aske was found guilty of treason and sentenced to be hanged, drawn and quartered; however this sentence was changed, some say at his own request, to that of being hanged in chains. The punishment occurred, or began at least, at Clifford's Tower in York on this date. Usually in the case of gibbeting, as the punishment was known, the culprit would be executed first, but reports state that this was not the case with Aske. He was wrapped in a metal cage and simply left to hang on the gibbet to die slowly from hunger, thirst and exposure, while birds pecked at his body. It is said that it took him a week in total to die, and his body was left to hang there for a further year afterwards.

Clifford's Tower, the main keep of York Castle, as it looks today. (Author's collection)

13 JULY 1535 During a service at Jervaulx Abbey on 11 July 1535, the abbot, Adam Sedbergh, had begun to preach a sermon confirming the supremacy of Henry VIII over the Church in England in the presence of Henry's emissary Sir Francis Bigod, when one of his monks, George Lazenby, interrupted him to announce that the Bishop of Rome had the first and most authority in all the world above all other bishops. These words being considered treasonable, Lazenby was arrested and taken to Middleham Castle where, on this date, he was tortured but refused to retract his statement, even having it written down and signing his name to it, as well as stating his intention to become a martyr, and claiming to have had visions of the Virgin Mary. He was taken to York Castle where, on 6 August, he received his wish in being sentenced to death. He was hanged at the Knavesmire soon afterwards.

14 JULY 1934 Mrs Clara Scott was attending a picnic on this date with her 14-year-old son and her husband, who was blind. As they walked from their home in Lower Ebor Street towards the Knavesmire, they attempted to cross Scarcroft Road and had just stepped from the curb when a car came into view from a crest in the road. Frank Parker, the driver of the car, honked his horn and this seems to have disoriented Mr Scott, as he grabbed the arm of his wife and child and attempted to run. However, instead of regaining the pavement, he headed straight at the front of the car, giving the driver no chance to avoid them. All three were struck, and Mrs Scott fell backwards, hitting her head on the kerb and dying almost instantly.

15 JULY 1835 At the small village of Kexby, on the outskirts of York, Thomas Robinson went on this night to visit a lady friend by the name of Palfreyman. A gamekeeper on Escrick Park, Robinson had a double-barrelled shotgun in his possession when he left, and shortly afterwards shots were heard, but further away than he should have reached in that time. When Robinson failed to return home, his friends became concerned and a search was made, whereupon he was discovered near a rabbit warren with his throat cut down to the bone. His gun was found some considerable distance away, and those who knew him said this was consistent with his behaviour when apprehending poachers. It seems he must have heard the gunshots, stowed his weapon and gone in pursuit. His outer clothing was also found discarded, the suggestion being that he had done so in order to move faster. Although a man named John Morley was arrested and tried for the murder, he was found not guilty. Several others were also arrested but no evidence could be found to charge them. The Robinson family seem to have been unlucky; the deceased man's older brother

had been shot dead in an accident a year previously. Thomas' younger brother Edward replaced him as gamekeeper on the estate, and later that year managed to shoot himself dead while reloading his gun.

16 JULY 1644 The end of the Siege of York was actually a fairly bloodless affair. After the Battle of Marston Moor, the city's position had become untenable. Prince Rupert of the Rhine and his army had marched south to meet up with the

Prince Rupert of the Rhine. (Author's collection)

main Royalist forces, and the Marquis of Newcastle, thoroughly demoralised, had marched his army away from the city, going into exile in Holland. Many of the citizens had taken the opportunity that the break in the siege had presented to escape the city and now there were said to be not 500 able-bodied men left to protect the place. The city was left in the hands of its governor, Sir Thomas Glenham, who sought terms with the besieging army. On this date he led his remaining men out through the Micklegate Bar and handed the city over to Lord Fairfax. Many of the besiegers – particularly in the Scottish Covenanter Army – wanted to ransack the place, but Fairfax, while giving them some opportunity to vent their desires, ordered that the churches, and particularly the minster with its priceless stained glass, should be left untouched. He appointed Sir Thomas Hoyle, a local man and a devout Puritan, as the new Lord Mayor to help rebuild the city. Hoyle would later be persuaded, as part of the Rump Parliament, to vote for the execution of King Charles I. One year, almost to the exact hour after that execution took place, Hoyle hanged himself in his Westminster apartments, apparently haunted by his decision.

17 JULY 1840 The Crown Court in York on this date heard the case of Hester Watson, a 40-year-old spinster who lived with her mother in the village of Flawith, just north of the city. On 29 May, her neighbour, Elizabeth Thompson, had heard noises coming from the house and, looking through the window, had seen Watson sitting on top of her mother and beating her head against the floor. Thompson ran to the village and returned with two men, William Gatenby and George Smith, as well as Smith's wife, and together they broke into the house, where they found the scene unchanged. Watson had tied a scarf around her mother's neck and was using it to lift her head from the floor and bang it back down repeatedly. The older woman was clearly dead already at this point. When George Smith tried to lift the woman off her mother's body, she cried out, 'Glory to God, I have done it!' She was found not guilty due to insanity and sent to an asylum.

18 JULY 1804 Benjamin Oldroyd, who was tried, convicted and hanged at York for the murder of his father, had cancer of the neck. On this date it was bleeding, so his mother had gone out to get some ointment to treat it. On her return she found that her husband had also gone out, but Benjamin said he did not know where. Shortly afterwards she went outside and found him dead, propped against a tree. At the inquest Mrs Oldroyd claimed that her husband had a rope around his neck when he was found, but Benjamin said he did not. A rope was found nearby, and a

post-mortem showed that the man had been hanged, but no corresponding rope marks were found on the tree, and the branches were considered too weak to have supported his weight anyway. After being found guilty of his murder, and sentenced to death, Benjamin protested his innocence to the very end, so never confessed to what had happened, but the conjecture was that the old man – who was infirm and had been in bed when his wife left – had complained once too often, and that his son had put the rope round his neck and hanged him from a roof beam above the bed.

19 JULY 1793 John Hoyland, a 77-year-old man from Attercliffe, near Sheffield, was prosecuted at the York Assizes on this date for a rather unusual crime. Hoyland had been a married man in his younger days, and had brought up a large family. By this time, however, he was living alone and tending to his farm. One day, two labourers passing by looked over into his fields and claimed to have seen him enjoying carnal pleasure with an ass. The offence was said to have taken place on the 15th, and four days later he found himself in court being sentenced to death for the crime of bestiality. Two other criminals were handed down the death sentence on the same day, one for robbery and one for sheep stealing, but both were reprieved while Hoyland's sentence was upheld. The sentence was carried out at the Knavesmire in York three weeks later.

20 JULY 1604 This week, the parish registers of York record the first burials of plague victims in the city for what would be the worst outbreak of bubonic plague in the history of the city. The outbreak had started in Newcastle 1603 and spread south, reaching Tadcaster and Wetherby by the end of that year. Stringent procedures were put in place to try to prevent it entering the city, including killing cats and dogs, which of course did nothing to prevent the spread of the rats, which carried fleas – the real carriers of the disease. As suspected cases started to emerge, victims were moved to tented settlements outside the city walls and elected officials began to flee the city to safer parts of the country. The disease ravaged the city, with nearly one quarter of the population said to have perished. The official death toll by the time the winter cold put an end to the outbreak was given as 3,512 persons.

21 JULY 1403 Although the death of Harry Hotspur on this date did not occur in York, he nonetheless was shortly to become a resident of the city, in spirit at least. Sir Henry Percy, to give him his proper name, is best remembered today for the role he plays in Shakespeare's *Henry IV, Part I*, where he is seen dying at the hands of

Statue of Sir Henry Percy, better known as Harry Hotspur, whose head was displayed on the Micklegate Bar to quell rumours that he was still alive. (Author's collection)

Prince Hal at the Battle of Shrewsbury. While he did indeed die in that battle, it is unlikely that Henry himself struck the fatal blow. Percy was buried in Shropshire, but rumours began to circulate that he was still alive, and so to scotch this gossip Henry IV had the body exhumed and displayed in the market place of Shrewsbury propped upright between two millstones. Then he had the body quartered and the four parts were sent around the kingdom, with the head being sent to York and displayed on a spike on the Micklegate Bar. Eventually, his wife was given permission to collect his remains, and he was once again given a proper Christian burial at York Minster.

22 JULY 1651 A strange and startling scene occurred on this night just outside York at the country home of a Peter Vavasor. A gentleman calling himself Tempest, but later identified as a minister's son named Richard Chamley, arrived at the house during the afternoon, claiming to be a messenger from Vavasor's father. He was invited into the house, but behaved in such an ungentlemanly and abusive manner that Vavasor declined to invite the man to stay the night and turned him out at around 7 p.m. At midnight, the house was surrounded by seven armed men on horseback, demanding entry. Vavasor blew a horn at an upstairs window to try to summon help but none came. The men claimed that they were hunting for Tempest who, they said, was trying to raise troops for the king against the Parliamentary forces. However, Vavasor recognised the voice of the one who had called himself Tempest among them. This was confirmed by others who had encountered the armed horsemen and it was believed that Tempest wanted to avenge himself on Vavasor for not offering him hospitality. The men broke down the windows and threatened to shoot their guns into the house before eventually saying that they would go away if given beer, a request to which Vavasor agreed. They then demanded oats for the horses but he said he had none and eventually they left.

23 JULY 1900 There were dramatic gasps of surprise in the Nisi Prius Court at York Castle on this date as a jury returned a verdict of not guilty against John Joe Arthur Chapman, a 15-year-old boy accused of sexual assault against an 8-year-old girl. The evidence against him had seemed so airtight that even the judge was moved, in his summing up, to state that, 'I am certain that the prisoner has done this at one time or another. Although he may escape at the hands of the jury, this boy has done it. He ought to be whipped, and if you (to the boy's father) take my advice, you will whip him.' It was reported that even the jury themselves seemed to be in approval of his words.

24 JULY 759 Oswulf ascended the throne as King of Northumbria in 758, after his father, Eadberht, who had ruled the kingdom peacefully for twenty years, abdicated in order to take holy orders and enter the monastery attached to the minster at York. His father having been a popular ruler, and his uncle being Ecgbert, the Archbishop at York, it was to be expected that Oswulf would have a long and successful reign. Sadly, this was not to be. A year after his coronation, on this date, he was murdered by members of his own household staff at a place called Methil Wongtun – thought likely to be the modern village of Market Weighton – which lies on the road between York and Hull. The exact details of the murder are not known, but it is likely that his killers were bribed by Aethelwald Moll who, despite not being of the royal line, seized the throne and later killed Oswulf's brother Oswine in battle in order to secure it.

25 JULY 1644 This is the date given for the death of two Catholic martyrs by the names of Boniface Kempe and Idlephonse Hesketh, whose real names appear to have been Francis Kipton and William Hanson. The two men were priests of the Benedictine order, and are said to have been taken at York during the English Civil War. The memoirs of Father Arthur Bell tell us that they were 'taken by parliament soldiers, and driven on foot before them in the heat of the summer, by which cruel and outrageous usage they were so heated and spent that they either forthwith or soon after died'.

26 JULY 1739 A young man by the name of Benjamin Barrack is said to have had a rather unfortunate accident. He had been sent by his master to retrieve his gun, which had been left in some place (where is not recorded). Benjamin, 15 years old at the time, dutifully went about his business and retrieved the weapon; however, he does not seem to have checked that it was in a safe condition, and on his way to return the gun to its owner, it discharged and a young woman, who appears to have sadly been in the wrong place at the wrong time, was shot dead on the spot. He was tried two days later at the assizes court and found guilty of manslaughter. His punishment was to be burned on the hand and imprisoned for two years.

27 JULY 1612 The trial of the Pendle Witches caused a great sensation in its day. Pendle is in Lancashire, and of the twelve women accused of witchcraft, eleven of them were tried at the assizes in Lancaster. However, one of the women, Jennet Preston, lived within the county of Yorkshire, and so was sent to York for her trial instead. On this date she was accused of the murder of a local landowner, Thomas

Lister of Westby Hall, through the use of witchcraft. Preston admitted to being a witch and to using magic and potions for the benefit of others in return for money, but she denied having caused Lister's death and pleaded not guilty. However, there was a belief at the time that when a murderer touched the body of their victim the body would bleed, and testimony was given to the court that Lister's body had indeed bled profusely when Preston came near to it. She was accordingly found guilty and hanged at the Knavesmire two days later.

28 JULY 1623 A wealthy landowner by the name of Fletcher was apparently wed to a much younger woman who had married him for his money. Despite their marriage, she carried on a dalliance with her former lover, a man named Ralph Raynard, who kept an inn on the road between Raskelf and Easingwolde, a few miles north of York. On May Day of 1623 Fletcher was murdered by Raynard, with the aid of another man named Mark Dunn. Mrs Fletcher laid in wait for her husband near Dawnay Bridge, and as he appeared on his way home from an assignment in the town of Huby, she appeared in order to halt him. As soon as he descended from his horse he was set upon by the two men, who drowned him. His body was then placed in a sack and buried in Raynard's garden. However, it seems that the guilt hung heavily on Raynard, who began to see visions of Fletcher calling on him to repent. One night his sister heard him confessing all in confidence to another man, and she ran to tell the local Justice of the Peace. The three were hanged at the Knavesmire on this date.

29 JULY 1904 Hearing sounds of quarrelling followed by an ominous silence, the neighbours of John Dalby in Alma Terrace decided to go to his house on this night to find out if there was any problem. Forcing the back door of the house, a tall man rushed out past them, shouting, 'I'll fetch a doctor', scaled the back wall and disappeared into the night. Inside the house they found Dalby lying on the floor in a pool of blood, with a deep gash in his throat. He was still alive, but after being rushed to the hospital, died the following day. Hearing that his son-in-law, Edmund Hall, had visited him that day, the police rushed to the railway station, where they found Hall preparing to board a train to Leeds. His shirt showed signs of having been recently washed, while bloodstains were found on other parts of his clothing. He was arrested and charged immediately with the attempted murder; the following day, this was changed to murder. Hall, who had recently lost his job, had apparently gone to the old man for money. Having been refused it, Hall had killed him and stolen his silver pocket watch. He was executed for the crime on 20 December that year.

York railway station in the early twentieth century. (Author's collection)

30 JULY 1644 York is a city synonymous with famous highwaymen, although they mostly plied their trade on the roads leading from London. An exception was Amos Lawson, a local man from Huddersfield, who made the Forest of Galtres – which surrounded York – his own territory. On this date, Lawson came to a sticky end at the gallows on the Knavesmire, where his execution is said to have been attended by between 8,000 and 9,000 locals, and contemporary reports state that the scene more resembled a fair for business and pleasure than a place of execution. Lawson had been arrested a few months earlier when he had laid in wait to rob a carriage, not realising that its occupant was none other than William Taylor, the Sheriff of Yorkshire.

31 JULY 1858 An enquiry commenced on this date into the conduct of a Mr Metcalfe, proprietor of a private asylum at Acomb House in York. Mrs Mary Turner, had separated from her husband, Liverpool bankruptcy official Charles Turner in 1857, after discovering that he was having an affair. In December of that year, she became convinced that her ex-husband was attempting to poison her and had acted in such a bizarre manner that doctors declared her insane and she was taken to the institution in question. There she is said to have undergone inhumane treatment, and twice escaped. On the second occasion, Metcalfe had found her in lodgings in York, broke

down the door of her room and dragged her naked from her bed, attempting to pull her into a cab in the street in that condition. When she complained, he told her that plenty of men had seen her naked before and suggested that she was of a promiscuous nature in front of several others. Mary Turner managed to have a Lunacy Commission held and was declared sane. An enquiry was held and such was the public outcry when they heard the treatment she had undergone that Metcalfe was forced out of business and ran away overseas, afraid that he was going to be prosecuted. He was indicted by a grand jury, and a bench warrant put out against him, but he was never apprehended.

AUGUST

St William's College. (Author's collection)

1 AUGUST 1853 An inquest held at York Hospital on this date was unable to deduce exactly how Robert Arrowsmith had died, although it was thought most likely that he had fallen while intoxicated and hit his head on the steps of York Minster. Arrowsmith had gone out to Clifton on the previous Saturday, 23 July, to collect manure on the high road. When he returned home he was highly intoxicated, his face was covered in red paint, his shirt collar was torn, and he had marks on his throat and bruising on his arms and legs. He complained to his wife that he had been abused by a man whose name she was later was unable to remember. He was attended by a doctor on the Tuesday of that week, and removed to the hospital on the Thursday, where he told the doctors he remembered falling on the minster steps. He died on the Sunday.

2 AUGUST 1830 This was the date of the Yarm Fair, and William Huntley of Crathorne was intending to attend the fair to make repayment of a debt, having recently come into some £85 in an inheritance. He was to be accompanied by his friend Robert Golesborough, who had purchased a gun the day before. Just after midnight, a gunshot was heard in the local area, and the following morning a large pool of blood was found by the side of the road. Huntley never appeared again, and Golesborough told people he had decided to try his luck in America. Although there was suspicion against the man, especially as he seemed to suddenly come into money himself, nothing could be proven until eleven years later when, in June 1841, a farmer named John Mellis in nearby Seamore discovered a quantity of human bones near a stream on his property. Among the bones was a skull with a distinctive projecting tooth, which Huntley had possessed. The skull also had a clear bullet hole; the victim had been shot through the head. Golesborough was tried for murder at the York Assizes in March 1842, but the jury were unable to say that he was guilty beyond reasonable doubt, and he was found not guilty.

3 AUGUST 1878 A group of Irish labourers were having some drinks in a public house close to the cattle market on this night. One of them, James Raftree, had had some family dispute with another man named James Boyne, and while drinking, Boyne and some other men entered the premises and asked Raftree's group to drink with them. They refused and an argument broke out which led to a fight. Raftree was knocked unconscious in the fight, and on coming round, he headed for home. As he passed down Long Close Lane, near Walmgate, Boyne came out of his own doorway with a revolver and shot at him, but the gun misfired. Another man, James Calpin, stepped in to stop Boyne from firing again, but Boyne ran back into his house and

shot at Raftree from an upstairs window. However, on this occasion the bullet missed and struck another man, Frank Conway. A friend of Boyne's, Conway later tried to claim that events had not occurred this way, that there had been no shooting in the street, and that Boyne had shot him accidentally while indoors. Nonetheless, Boyne was found guilty and sentenced to one year's hard labour.

4 AUGUST 1804 The *York Herald* reported on the trial of Jonathan Ellis, who was found guilty at York Castle of raping a 15-year-old girl named Elizabeth Widdison. Ellis, who was hanged for the crime the following week, approached the girl on the pretence of asking for directions, then chased her down the road and forced himself on her. He had been arrested by the victim's own father, who had tracked him down to a nearby inn after he found out what had happened. At court he described how his wife had fetched a midwife to examine the girl, that he had been present during the examination and that he had known his daughter was telling the truth about what had happened when 'he immediately perceived upon the countenance of his wife the visible marks of sorrow'.

5 AUGUST 1878 Two men were committed for trial on this date after a street brawl ended in death. The argument between Alexander Kelly and Benjamin Hartley had begun when the latter accused Kelly of stealing money from his wife. The argument occurred in a shop owned by Anthony Garvey in Walmgate. Hartley punched Kelly during the initial altercation, but before a fight could break out, a policeman separated them. Later the two men came to blows again when they were seen apparently trying to strangle each other. Again they were separated. Eventually, at the urging of a man named Henry Collins, Kelly attacked Hartley in the street and the two men ended up in a brawl, during which the rear of Kelly's head struck a paving stone, causing a 4in fracture to the skull; he never regained consciousness and died the following day. Hartley was sentenced to a week's imprisonment for the manslaughter, but Collins was sentenced to three months for aiding and abetting and for instigating the fight.

6 AUGUST 1759 This was the date intended for the execution of Eugene Arum, who had been arrested at Lynn in Norfolk for a murder committed in Knaresborough some fifteen years earlier, after which he had absconded. On the morning of the execution, Arum was called from his bed in York Castle prison to have his irons removed. His reply was that he was very weak and could not move. The guards called for a doctor and entered the cell, whereupon they found that Arum had attempted

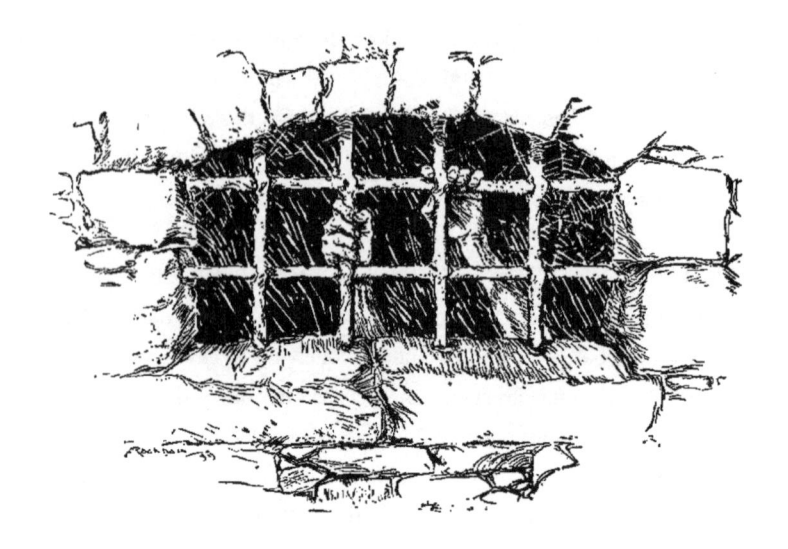

suicide during the night by slitting his wrists with a razor he had smuggled into the cell. He had made two cuts, but neither was deep enough so that, while he had bled profusely, it was not enough to endanger his life. He was helped to the gallows and executed as planned. Afterwards a note was found in the cell in which he explained that he had wanted to die on his own terms, and not those of the state.

7 AUGUST 1679 The execution of 82-year-old Father Nicholas Postgate at the Knavesmire on this date was the strange consequence of a plot conceived far away. The law by which practising Catholic priests were put to death, introduced by Elizabeth I nearly 100 years earlier, was still in force. Despite this, Postgate – who had been ordained into the Catholic Church as a young man – had managed to live to a ripe old age. For many years he had been maintained by noble families around York who secretly followed the Catholic faith, and for the previous twenty years had acted as a missionary, travelling the North York Moors and never remaining too long in one place. However, he fell foul of a plan by Titus Oates to implicate the Church in a plot to assassinate King Charles II. Together with another man, Israel Tonge, Oates had fabricated the plot, but persuaded a magistrate, Sir Edmund Godfrey, to investigate it. When Godfrey was found murdered, it was blamed on this plot, and his servant John Reeves swore to avenge his death. Travelling in the North, he came across a farmer called Matthew Lyth who had spoken out against Protestantism, and decided he was involved. Lyth had a baby son, and Reeves learned he was to baptised into the Catholic faith, so he arranged for the farm to be raided during the ceremony, which Postgate was officiating.

8 AUGUST 1825 Thomas Fisher, a miller at Newton-on-Ouse on the outskirts of York, died on this morning as a consequence of an altercation a few days earlier. Fisher had been drinking in the George and Dragon public house (which is now the Dawnay Arms) when his wife entered and, seeing him with a group of men of whom she disapproved, asked him what he was doing drinking with such blackguards. One of the men, Joseph Wilson, took offence, and Fisher set to defending his wife, resulting in a scuffle. The men were separated and Fisher was pulled away into the kitchen while Wilson stormed out. He then removed his shirt and went round to the back of the establishment where Fisher was outside the kitchen door. Asking the man if he was ready, he walked straight up and punched him in the face, knocking him insensible. Fisher recovered briefly the following day, but his condition steadily deteriorated until his death, which doctors ascribed to the result of a concussion.

9 AUGUST 1892 Thomas Shopland, a 24-year-old fishmonger's assistant from Newcastle, signed a bond on a loan for a friend at Christmas of 1891. His friend promptly absconded with the money, leaving Shopland with heavy repayments each month; at the beginning of this month he had been hit with a demand for an amount that would leave him virtually destitute. He was said to have been in a deep depression about this for some considerable time, and on this evening he arrived in York and took a room at the Commercial Hotel in Tanner Row. The following morning, the housemaid was unable to enter the room and so called the manager, who opened the door. Inside he found Shopland lying on the bed with the bed sheets covering his face, and with his throat cut across so deeply that his head was almost severed. In his left hand he held an open razor, with which he had clearly performed the deed. There was also an empty bottle of laudanum at his side. On the table he had left a note that merely gave his identity for whoever found him.

10 AUGUST 1767 On this date, Ann Sowerby of Whitby was burned at the stake on the Knavesmire for the murder of her husband. She had apparently entered into a murder pact with her lover that both would dispose of their respective spouses so that they could be together. Prior to her execution, she confessed that her paramour, John Douglas, had bought nux vomica, the poison known today as strychnine, and given her some to give to her husband. She could not go through with it and so burned the poison, but after Douglas went ahead and disposed of his wife, she agreed to go ahead and this time he provided her with arsenic, which she mixed with some curds and gave her husband for breakfast. She was strangled prior to burning to spare her the worst of the flames.

11 AUGUST 1582 The sentence of death passed down on William Lacy at York Castle on this date must almost have come as a relief. Since his arrest a month earlier, Lacy is said to have been kept in an underground dungeon, weighted down with heavy chains at all times, and regularly tortured. After being twice married and widowed, Lacy had travelled to Rome to study for the Catholic priesthood, and was ordained in 1581. He then travelled back to England and was arrested while attending Mass in York at the home of one Thomas Bell. He was found to be in possession of items blessed by the Pope and when instructed to proclaim Queen Elizabeth as Supreme Governor of the Church he refused to do so. This was enough for him to be found guilty of treason, and he was placed in a tiny prison cell along with another priest, Richard Kirkman, who had been arrested three days earlier. Both men were hanged, drawn and quartered eleven days later. On being sentenced he is said to have replied, 'It is only paying the common debt a little sooner. We will go into the house of the Lord.'

12 AUGUST 1820 The execution at York of Thomas Pickersgill for highway robbery on this date reveals the story of a rather brutal man. He had been drinking in a public house near Wakefield with a Squire Ramsden, and had offered to accompany the other man home but had been declined. On leaving the establishment, Ramsden had heard boots behind him, and as he turned around he was knocked to the ground, before someone began kicking his head repeatedly and with force. The assailant was shouting at him to stay quiet and he recognised the voice as that of Pickersgill. He decided his best course of action was to lie as still as possible, while the man rummaged about his person and took his purse and pocketbook. After his assailant had left, he called out for help, but instead Pickersgill returned and with the words, 'damn thee, thou art not quiet yet, but if I have not given enough, I will do,' began to kick him once again in the head, ribs, and genitals. Ramsden cried out to him, 'thou hast got my money, let me die quietly,' and Pickering swore at him. At this point Ramsden passed out, while Pickersgill, apparently believing him dead, finally left off his attack and departed.

13 AUGUST 1895 On this morning York Castle Prison witnessed the ending to a story that was said to have shocked the nation. Robert Hudson had been a furniture salesman in Nottingham until the previous May when, as a consequence of getting himself in financial difficulty, he moved his family to Helmsley, a village north of York. He had been married for eighteen months and had one child, a daughter. The other inhabitants all spoke of his obvious affection and love for his family, and how he and his wife would at all times walk hand-in-hand and behave more like a pair of romantic lovers than husband and wife. However, it seems that this was an act on his part, and he was planning to marry a rich woman to end his financial troubles. On 5 June, he had bought a spade and, attaching it to his bicycle, rode out to Roper Moor, where the next day a workman stumbled on a large hole he had dug. Three days later he went out to the moor with his wife and child, supposedly for a pleasant walk. When he returned, he told his landlady that his wife had gone with the child to visit an aunt near Hovingham. He then left for Nottingham, writing a letter to his sister in which he stated that his wife had left him. Suspicious, she went to visit the landlady, and a search was made. When the workman told them of the hole he had found, it was located and inside were the bodies of the two females, their throats cut savagely. On this date he was hanged at York, and was said to have shown almost no emotion regarding the murders from the time of his arrest until the night before his execution, when he finally broke down after a visit from his family.

14 AUGUST 1850 William Ross was tried at York, although his crime occurred in a village near Ashton-under-Lyne in Lancashire. The trial took place over two days in July, during which evidence was heard that Ross had charged some members of his wife's family with burglary, whereupon his mother-in-law had been sent to prison. Ross had also been heard to say that he would have revenge on the family, and shortly afterwards his wife became sick and died. An examination showed arsenic poisoning, and arsenic was also found on Ross's watch fob, but he claimed that his sister-in-law, Martha Buckley, had asked him to buy it, which she refuted. Evidence seemed to point to Ross as the murderer, as while his wife was ill he was heard to make plans to go to America, and on her death he immediately set about collecting a large sum of money from funeral clubs to which she had belonged. He was consequently found guilty and sentenced to death. However, he continued to loudly claim innocence, and later it was discovered that Martha Buckley had indeed attempted to buy the arsenic a few days earlier, and had been heard to ask Ross to buy it for her. It was suggested that there was a great deal more mitigating evidence, but that Ross had not had the resources to pay investigators to discover it. On 10 August, the date appointed for his hanging at York Castle, a stay of execution was given for one week, and on this date all the evidence was placed before the Home Secretary. He, however, found no reason to change the verdict, and ordered that the execution go ahead. Petitions were quickly got up for a commutation of the sentence, but Ross was hanged on the appointed day, still claiming innocence even from the gallows. The case became a cause célèbre, and resulted in many calls and even discussion in Parliament with regard to abolishing the death sentence.

15 AUGUST 1818 An interesting story appeared in several newspapers that a clothier of the name of Slater had disappeared – in a very mysterious manner – about forty years earlier. On this day his son, a manufacturer at Yeadon, met an aged man named Joseph Royston begging alms at Keighley. The old man first told Mr Slater that about forty years ago he had killed a person named Slater and buried him in the corner of a cornfield, about 12 miles below York. He subsequently, however, said that it was not by him that Slater was killed, but that he was killed, and he could point out the spot where he was buried. Royston, Slater and the constable of Yeadon travelled to the field and searched in several places, including a churchyard, but no trace of the body could be found. Suspicion still existed that the man was telling the truth but had thought better of producing a body, which could have resulted in his prosecution for murder.

16 AUGUST 946 This is the date of the coronation of Eadred, the English king who brought Northumbria, and its capital city York, into the Kingdom of England. At the time the Northumbrian throne was in the hands of the Viking Erik Bloodaxe. Erik had won the throne from another Viking leader, Olaf Sihtricson, who was the godson of Eadred's brother. Accordingly, he brought his army north, where he is said to have laid waste to the kingdom over the following years. The *Anglo-Saxon Chronicle* tells us that in 948 he overtook Erik at York, where 'there was great slaughter made, and the King was so wroth that he would fain return with his force and lay waste the land withal, but when the Council of Northumbria understood that, they abandoned Erik and compromised the deed with Eadred'. Erik returned and reigned for two further years beginning in 952, before being finally ejected from the kingdom.

17 AUGUST 1839 After a hard day of labouring, the inmates of the Marygate Workhouse looked forward to a steaming bowl of soup as their reward. However, within moments of having completed their repast, several complained of feeling unwell, and as time went on more fell victim to the mysterious malady, including two persons living in the same street who had been given some of the soup by the workhouse master. One woman was reported to have turned black and others were showing alarming symptoms. Doctors were called in and treated all the victims, although it was reported that four had died. It was strongly suspected that the soup had been deliberately poisoned, although no perpetrator was ever discovered. One member of the board of governors of the workhouse suggested that the lack of potatoes in the soup had left it too rich for the stomachs of the poor.

Now the York Post Office Club, this building housed the Marygate Workhouse. (Author's collection)

18 AUGUST 1670 Beningbrough Hall is now a popular resort hotel on the outskirts of York, but in 1670 it was the ancestral home of a nobleman named Earle who, being a Catholic, was under threat of arrest. He made a plot with his housekeeper Marion to hide his valuables in the home of his gamekeeper, her lover, Martin Giles. However, the steward of the house, Philip Laurie, got wind of this and resolved to steal the valuables with the help of a local poacher named William Vasey. The pair first had to rid themselves of Marion, so Vasey hid out on the route of her nightly walk and, jumping from behind a tree, dragged her to the river and drowned her. Laurie and Vasey then went to the gamekeeper's cottage to remove the valuables, but Giles was awake and surprised them, knocking Vasey unconscious. Vasey was arrested, charged with Marion's murder and eventually executed on this date. Suspicion fell on Laurie but nothing could be proved; however, Earle's wife dismissed him from their service, whereupon he threatened her with a gun, and then afterwards removed himself to his own quarters and used the gun to take his own life.

19 AUGUST 1900 Early on this morning, at around 1 a.m., PC Hodgson of the York Police came across Jessie Allen, a 34-year-old woman, lying on the ground in a passage of St Margaret's Street, screaming and abusing passers-by, as a result of which she had caused a large disturbance and a crowd had gathered. Allen was taken into custody and brought up before the police court the following Wednesday, where she was fined for being drunk and disorderly. What makes this case of interest is that at the police court hearing, the judge was on familiar terms with the prisoner, on account of it being the sixty-seventh time she had appeared before him on the same charge.

20 AUGUST 1869 A group of young boys, mostly aged around 10 or 11, were on the city walls on this day between Walmgate Bar and the Red Tower, above a patch of grass where some Gypsies had camped outside the wall. They were shouting taunts at the Gypsies, and throwing stones down into the camp, one of which broke a pitcher. One of the Gypsies, William Smith, managed to mount the wall with the aid of some bricks, and began to chase the lads with a stick. As he did, one of the boys, William Durham, slipped and fell from the wall into the yard of the Walmgate church school. Falling head first, he was knocked unconscious and expired a few minutes afterwards. At the inquest the jury heard that Smith had aimed a blow at the boy but had not struck him, and were asked to consider if this had caused the fall. The death was eventually declared to be accidental, but the jury expressed their view that the camp outside the walls was a nuisance and ought not to be allowed.

Walmgate Bar in the early nineteenth century. (Author's collection)

21 AUGUST 1138 On the day before the Battle of the Standard, troops raised in York by the 70-year-old Archbishop Thurstan camped in Thirsk (to the north of the city) and sent Robert de Brus and Bernard de Balliol, two Norman noblemen who had sworn allegiance to the Scottish King David I, to meet with David as he approached from the north. They went with a promise of aiding David if he would withdraw from the field, but, while it is not recorded exactly what was said at the meeting, it is certain that things did not go well, and de Brus returned and immediately withdrew his homage to the Scotsman. The following day the armies met, the English under a standard built by Archbishop Thurstan, consisting of a mast mounted on a cart, bearing the holy sacrament and the standards of the minsters of York, Beverley and Ripon. The Scots attacked first with Galwegian spearmen, who charged headlong into the battle only to be met by the swords of dismounted knights supported by phalanxes of archers and slaughtered. This left David's army in disarray, and while the Scottish king tried to stand and fight, his men began to flee and he had no choice but to follow. The battle was concluded in three hours with heavy losses on the Scottish side.

Monument marking the site of the Battle of the Standard. (Author's collection)

22 AUGUST 1572 The Rising of the North was one of several attempts to restore the Catholic Church in the North after Henry VIII's Dissolution of the Monasteries. In this case the attempt was led by two nobles: Thomas Percy, the 7th Earl of Northumberland, and Charles Neville, the 6th Earl of Westmorland. Their aim was to remove Elizabeth I from the throne and replace her with Mary, Queen of Scots, who was recognised by the Catholic Church as the rightful ruler on account of Elizabeth's birth being considered illegitimate. The rebellion took place in late 1569 and was put down by the Earl of Sussex, who marched from York to rout the rebels at Clifford Moor. The two earls fled to Scotland, but Percy was captured by the Scottish regent, the Earl of Morton, who sold him to the English government for £2,000 three years later. Percy was conducted back to York, where Elizabeth had him publicly executed by beheading outside All Saints' church, Pavement, on this date.

Sir Thomas Percy, 7th Earl of Northumberland was executed outside All Saints' church, Pavement, in York.

23 AUGUST 1536 The Dissolution of the Monasteries under Henry VIII had begun with the suppression of all religious houses under the value of £200, and by this date the larger institutions were also being threatened, leading to widespread unrest among the general populace. On this date, a theatrical production based on the story of St Thomas the Apostle was being performed in the city streets when some of the language of the show roused the people up into what was described as an 'evil and seditious rising'. Henry, on being informed of these events, ordered the Lord Mayor to arrest any 'papists' who likewise used seditious language in any future interludes based on the Bible.

24 AUGUST 1453 Heworth Moor saw a minor skirmish on this date that has been described as the first engagement of the Wars of the Roses. The Neville and Percy families, the two most important houses in the North, had been feuding for years, and on this date Thomas Neville returned across the moor towards Sheriff Hutton after his wedding to Maude Stanhope, the heir to the fortune of Baron Ralph de Cromwell. Years earlier, during the reign of Henry V, the Percys had been stripped of two estates which had been given to the Cromwell family, and it now seemed that these might be given in dowry to Neville; this was an insult the Percys could not bear.

The remains of Sheriff Hutton Castle, one of the main residences of the Neville family. A Neville wedding party were returning here when they were attacked by an army raised by the Percys. After Richard Neville was killed at the Battle of Barnet, the castle was given to Richard, Duke of Gloucester, who made it his main place of residence until his coronation as King Richard III. (Author's collection)

As such Thomas Percy, Lord Egremont, one of the younger members of the Percy clan, raised an army said to be close to 5,000 men and laid in wait to massacre the entire wedding party. In fact, while it is recorded that the two parties faced each other off, and many threats were made on both sides, it is less clear whether any actual fighting or loss of life actually occurred.

25 **AUGUST 1825** An inquest held at the County Hospital in York over three days ended on this date with a verdict of manslaughter being returned against Michael Bell, who had been involved in an affray with a man named John Dalby in Coney Street a few weeks earlier. During the fight, Bell had struck Dalby across the head with a walking stick and Dalby had ended up insensible in hospital. He had appeared to recover, and left hospital of his own accord, but had collapsed while milking his cows a day later and was readmitted. He died two days before this date. After considerable evidence had been heard, the jury finally came to the conclusion that Bell had been responsible for the death, but when the constable attempted to take him into custody to stand trial it was found that, realising that the evidence was going against him, Bell had absconded.

26 AUGUST 1932 Mr Plumer, the proprietor of a boarding house in York, entered one of the bedrooms where an occupant had arrived the previous day, giving no name, and had not checked out. In the room he found the man dead, with a gunshot wound to his temple. A gun with one chamber discharged was found near the body. It was obvious that the man had committed suicide, but what was intriguing was that before having done so, he had taken care to destroy anything that might serve to identify him. The only clues were a gunmetal watch that bore the name of a Dublin jeweller, a library book that had had the name of the library itself torn out, and a locked attaché case on which the letter S had been scratched in one corner. It wasn't until the following week that a bank book, which had been torn up and placed inside the chimney, was dislodged by wind; from the counterfoils the police were able to identify the man as George Shaw of Llangollen, who had been managing a hotel in that town and appeared to have been recently involved in some financial irregularities.

27 AUGUST 1869 Mark Darrell had been a police officer in Stockton-upon-Tees and was hurt in the line of duty in an incident that had left him paralysed and insensible. As a result he was admitted to the North Riding Lunatic Asylum in York, and on this date one of the attendants, William Tracey, was instructed to bathe him. Tracey took Darrell into the bathroom and lifted him into the bath, turning on the hot water taps, but found that the cold taps had no water. Tracey then left, leaving two inmates to watch the man while he fetched a shirt. He returned later, when the bath was around half full. When he lifted Darrell out of the bath, several people noted that his legs were very red, and later that day he was found sitting with his trousers above his knees, moaning. It was found that his legs were badly scalded and he was taken to the infirmary where the scalds were treated, but an infection had set in and less than a week later he died. Tracey was convicted of manslaughter on the grounds of having left the man unattended, which was against the rules of the asylum, and also of not having tested the temperature of the water.

28 AUGUST 1951 George Craze, a 24-year-old married father of two and a Second World War veteran from Leeds, gave up his job on August Bank Holiday weekend and over the next few days was seen various times in Scarborough and other places in Yorkshire. On this date he and another man, 20-year-old Kenneth Williams, checked into a hotel in York and went out to a public house together. Becoming quite drunk, Williams became jealous because Craze was getting more attention from the women present. The two men argued, and when they left the pub, Williams suddenly attacked his companion. Craze apparently made no attempt to defend himself, but pleaded with the man to stop, and then ran off down a lane which led to the River Ouse. Here Williams attacked him again, kicking him under the chin, then picking him up and throwing him to the ground three times. Some women arrived, pleading with him to stop, and a Hungarian man felt Craze's pulse but believed him dead. They then went to get a policeman, but when they returned Craze was no longer there: Williams would only say that he was gone. Craze's body was found at 1 a.m. the next day in the river near North Street. Williams was later said to have stopped a man on the Ouse Bridge and asked him to punch him in the face before he handed himself in to the police, presumably to make it look as if Craze had put up more of a fight. He was found guilty of manslaughter on the grounds that it could not be proved that Craze was not already dead before being thrown in the river.

29 AUGUST 1801 Edward Hughes was a private in the 18th Light Dragoons, and was riding to York on 30 May. While passing a field near Easingwold, he called out to a young girl, Mary Brown, who was working the fields, asking her the time and how far it was to York. When she replied, he called her a damned liar, climbed off his horse and took hold of her by the throat, then ripped at her clothing and raped her. As he attempted to catch his horse, she cried out and a pair of brothers called Driffield came to her aid, but Hughes drew his gun and threatened to shoot them. On the week of Hughes' trial, some of his fellow soldiers claimed that the girl's father had brought them to York Castle, where in a nearby inn he explained that his daughter would drop her claims if they paid her £50, and also gave him £14 as a commission. The soldiers replied that they did not have enough money, but would speak to their commanding officer. They stated that Mary was in the room while this transaction was discussed, and the judge at the trial told the jury that if they believed this testimony, then they must find the accused not guilty. Apparently they did not, because he was found guilty as charged and was hanged at the Knavesmire on this date.

30 AUGUST 1893 A verdict of manslaughter was returned by the York coroner on this date against Frances Priestley, the grandmother of a child, Harriet Spence, whose mother had left the girl in her care as she was in service. At the time of her death, Harriet was 15 months old and was said to have weighed around 10.5lbs – around half the weight expected for a child that age. Several medical professionals testified to having visited the child and found her severely neglected at various times, while neighbours stated that Mrs Priestley would often leave her for days without food or without changing her clothes or cleaning her. The cause of death was given as exhaustion as a result of extreme neglect.

31 AUGUST 1885 George O'Grady, a shoemaker, resided in Francis Street with his common-law wife Priscilla Hodgson, and returned home from work on this night somewhat the worse for drink. The two fell into an argument, which continued as they drank, being seen in several public houses. Later, when passing along Black Horse Passage, off Fossgate, the argument became violent and O'Grady pulled a knife from his pocket and made several attempts to cut the woman's throat. She managed to fend off his attack, although sustained severe injuries to her neck and hand and lost a great deal of blood. She was taken to York County Hospital, where she made a full recovery. On his arrest, O'Grady stated that he 'wished he killed the bitch' and that he had meant to murder her. He was committed for trial at the assizes, but hanged himself in his cell on 25 September.

SEPTEMBER

Originally a wooden structure, this stone bridge stands in the location of the original crossing over the River Derwent, around which the Battle of Stamford Bridge raged. (Author's collection)

1 SEPTEMBER 1821 On this date, five executions were set to take place at York Castle, conducted by William Curry, who remained York's official hangman for thirty-three years despite his apparent incompetence at the job. On this occasion he arranged things perfectly, lining all five men up to receive the drop with a single pull of the lever. Unfortunately, he failed to stand sufficiently clear of the trapdoors. As they opened an anguished cry went up from the crowd as they saw a body fall to the ground and assumed that the rope had broken. This was followed by a huge cheer when they realised that the body was none other than Curry himself.

2 SEPTEMBER 1816 The newspapers on this date reported on the death of William Ward, the latest twist in a tale that occupied the chattering classes of York for much of the second half of the year. It was the case of Elizabeth Ward, a 17-year-old girl who had been found guilty of attempting to poison her sister, apparently with no motive. Her sister had become very ill and had gone to the local druggist, who gave her an emetic to induce vomiting. He had then preserved the vomit and sent it to be tested where it was found to contain arsenic. Elizabeth had purchased arsenic from him the previous day, and this was the evidence on which she was convicted. She was tried just seven days after the crime was committed and sentenced to death, but many petitions were put forward by the public, who were against executing a girl so young, and there were several stays of execution while the arguments were heard. William was Elizabeth's cousin and stated that he would hang himself if the sentence were carried out. After yet another stay, but no reprieve, he carried out his threat. Eventually her sentence was commuted to transportation, and later to ten years in an experimental institution designed to rehabilitate young female offenders.

3 SEPTEMBER 1839 When Elizabeth Sweeting died in the workhouse in Whitby on this date, it was the end of a story which stretched back several months and began in the parish of St Olave's in York. The young lady had been in service with a family there, but when she fell pregnant her position became untenable, and she was admitted to the Marygate Workhouse. As she was originally from Whitby, an order was obtained for her removal to the workhouse there instead, but in the meantime her confinement came on and she could not be moved. She gave birth on 1 August, and on the 3rd she requested her removal to Whitby, but was told she was not yet strong enough. Here accounts differ, as the workhouse records state that she insisted on her removal on the 7th, although she told people in Whitby that she had been forced to go. She also complained of being worked too hard at York,

and that she had been badly treated and made to stand and given no food or hot drinks during her delivery. In Whitby, the overseer of the workhouse could not be found, and Henry Lupton, who had brought her from York, ended up walking her around the town for nearly an hour and a half before they found the home of the assistant overseer. The staff of the Whitby institution made a number of complaints: the girl was inadequately dressed for her journey; her clothes were almost indecent; her shoes had no soles or heels so that she had been walking in her stockinged feet, and she was undernourished. The overseer also pointed out the illegality of her being removed while the suspension of her removal order had not been lifted. She also had breast problems, most likely mastitis, which were treated daily by a doctor during her time in Whitby, and may have ultimately been the cause of her death.

4 SEPTEMBER 1811 James Whitehead was said to be an uneducated man of intemperate habits, and had formed an attachment to fellow servant Ann Ochleton, who did not return his affection. This drove him into a rage and he stated that he would kill her if she ever married anyone but him. As a result she left the service of their mutual employer Mr Brown, and went to live at the home of her Aunt Jane. On this date the two women were out walking near to Jane's home when Whitehead appeared and started to walk alongside them. Ann told him to leave and he did so but returned shortly afterwards. When told to leave again, he took out a knife, threw Ann to the ground and inflicted a severe cut to her throat. Despite her wounded state she wrested the knife from his hands and threw it into some bushes. She then managed to run away and a man named Isaac Ellard prevented Whitehead from chasing her. Whitehead reportedly said to him, 'I'll have her life if possible. I know I'll be hanged for her, so I'll go to the gallows and be hanged like a dog!'

5 SEPTEMBER 1774 The body of Elizabeth Rambourne was discovered in a cellar belonging to a Captain John Bolton of the 1st Regiment of the West Riding Militia, at Bulmer, near Castle Howard. It seemed that she had been killed around two weeks previously. Bolton had, by all accounts, taken the young girl into his care as an orphan but had later seduced her, and she became pregnant. To prevent his wife and family from discovering this, he strangled the girl with a cord tied around a soldier's fife. After the crime was discovered, and Bolton sentenced to death, he hanged himself in his cell at York Castle before the sentence could be carried out. The case became famous as a result of a popular song of the time, which recounted events from Bolton's point of view. In the song title, and in popular legend, his victim's name is given as Elizabeth Rainbow.

6 SEPTEMBER 1888 John Hartas was the victim of a violent highway robbery when, while driving a flock of sheep from York to Malton on this date, he passed a man named James Clarke lying by the roadside, who requested his assistance. Afterwards he agreed to pay the man to help him take the sheep on along the road, but they then ran into two other men and a woman whom his new helper seemed to know. In fact – unknown to Hartas – the woman was Clarke's wife, and the others were his accomplices. Clarke told Hartas that he would go off with them, and asked for some of the money promised. As soon as Hartas busied himself with finding the money, the four of them rushed him, knocking him to the ground. One then sat on his chest while another covered his mouth to prevent him crying out. Knowing from his actions where his money was kept, they robbed him of all he had. Hartas arrived in Malton the following day and informed the local policeman what had happened; the culprits were soon rounded up and arrested.

7 SEPTEMBER Whip-Ma-Whop-Ma Gate In the centre of York, there is a tiny street that turns off Pavement and runs to the beginning of Colliergate. It is 36m long, and as such is the shortest 'named' street in the city. The name of the street is Whip-Ma-Whop-Ma Gate and where that name came from is an oft-asked question in the city. The gate part is easy to explain: most of the city streets are suffixed '-gate', and this derives from the Viking word 'gata', which meant 'to walk' or 'a path' and is the same word from which 'gait' for a person's stride is derived. As to the unusual first part, it is said to derive from 'whit-nour-what-nour', a medieval expression roughly corresponding to 'neither one thing nor the other'. It is said that the name changed to the modern spelling in the fifteenth and sixteenth centuries, when it was the location of the stocks and whipping post for petty criminals. However, ask a local and you are as likely to be told that it was once a location where it was legal to beat your wife on a Sunday if she had been troublesome or a nag during the week, to teach her the error of her ways. There is no evidence that this was ever the case, but it makes for an interesting tale.

8 SEPTEMBER 1875 Thomas Thompson, a cabinetmaker, was driving his cart from his shop in Peter Lane into Market Street when some incident occurred in which a barrel ended up under the wheels of his cart. As a result, both Thompson and a Market Street trader named Henry Pratt ended up taking the other to court for assault. According to Pratt, Thompson drove the cart into his boy, who was carrying the barrel, and it rolled under the wheels. According to Thompson, the boy rolled it there deliberately. The result was an altercation between the two inside Pratt's shop, during which Pratt claimed Thompson struck him twice with a whip, and Thompson claimed that Pratt seized him by the collar and struck him several times on the head, causing it to bleed in three places. The court dismissed both cases, whereupon a Mr Wilkinson, lawyer for one of the defendants, caused uproar in the court, accusing the Lord Mayor of dismissing a case of his without allowing him to speak for the second time in a single week. It was some time before the court could be brought back to order.

9 SEPTEMBER 1915 Private Harry MacDonald was a cook in the 14th Service Battalion of the East Yorkshire Regiment stationed at Ousethorpe, and his wife Charlotte took lodgings nearby in Pocklington at the home of a couple named Rodgers, who ran a fish and chip shop. They had not been married long, and seemed happy for a while, but Mrs Rodgers stated that a few weeks before this date they had argued, and things had been tense since. On this night MacDonald visited his wife and enticed her to go away with him, but she refused. Without warning he shouted that he had something for her, drew a razor and slashed through her throat before doing the same to himself. Mrs MacDonald is said to have slumped across Mrs Rodgers' lap and died very quickly from loss of blood. Private MacDonald ran from the house and collapsed in the front yard, but survived his wound. In a strange turn of events, at the inquest MacDonald was confronted by a woman named Bridget McCartney, who stated that his name was in fact John McCartney, and that he had married her sixteen years earlier, and left her some two years before. She asserted that they were still legally married. Documentation proved this to be the case, and so he was tried at York Assizes under his real name. Despite pleading insanity, he was found guilty and hanged at Wakefield on 15 December.

10 SEPTEMBER 1944 Returning from a night bombing raid on the shipyards at Octeville in France, the crew of a Halifax bomber operated by Free French forces was coming in for a landing at RAF Elvington, a few miles east of York. A regular part of the bomb-aimer's job was to check all the lamp indicators to see that all bombs had been dropped and none remained. He had reported to the pilot that this was the case, but was unaware that one of the bombs had become lodged in the bomb doors. As the aircraft hit the runway, this bomb became dislodged, fell to the ground and exploded. Six of the crew were killed, but the pilot was thrown clear of the wreckage.

11 SEPTEMBER 1893 Robert Wood was a former soldier who had served with distinction in the Royal Artillery and was among the first to enter Sebastopol following the famous siege during the Crimean War. On retirement, he had taken on the role of schoolmaster at York Castle. However, in later years he became prone to dementia, and on 10 September he left his house only partly dressed and apparently wandered aimlessly for nearly twenty-four hours, before collapsing from exhaustion and the effects of exposure. He was found dead in a field in Barlby, having travelled some 12 miles from his home in York. Due to his exemplary service, he was buried with full military honours.

12 SEPTEMBER 1860 On this morning, John Bradley was sent by his father from his home in St Saviourgate to deliver a letter to his uncle in Hungate. The man was not home but his daughter opened the letter and found that it was a suicide note, and contained an instruction to look in his pocket to find the reasons. The girl quickly located a policeman, who visited the house and found the boy's father – also called John – lying on the bed, still breathing but in an insensible state, with an empty bottle of laudanum and a glass with the dregs still in the bottom beside him. He had purchased the poison the day before, but had apparently only consumed it after sending his son on the errand. Doctors attempted to resuscitate him, but he died two hours later. In his pocket was a letter from his wife, informing him that she could not live with his drinking any more, which had consumed all of their money and left herself and her children in rags, and so had gone away to find a better position in life.

13 SEPTEMBER 1873 The *York Herald* included a story on this day of a farmer on his way to market in York, who had brought a basket of butter to the railway station in Shipton. He waited at the side of the platform while a goods train rattled through the station in the direction of York, and then began to cross the rails behind it, failing to notice that a second train was coming through at high speed in the other direction. The train clipped him and he fell to the ground, his head crossing the track so that he was entirely decapitated by the wheels of the train passing over his neck.

14 SEPTEMBER 1855 A great deal of shock was expressed in the city regarding an assault and robbery that occurred on this date in one of the most public streets of the city. A man named William Pollard was turning from Spurriergate into Market Street when he was tripped from behind and, as he fell, his head was struck with an iron bar. He became aware of three men who had gathered around him and began to kick at him repeatedly until he lost consciousness. On coming round, he realised that he had been robbed of all his valuables and money. He managed to crawl on his hands and knees into Parliament Street, where a policeman found him. He was examined by doctors and found to have two broken ribs and severe swelling on the back of his head, but was lucky to have survived the beating.

15 SEPTEMBER 1892 William Cooper, a traveller in the employment of a grocer's business with premises in Coney Street, had set out this morning to make deliveries in the Helmsley district. While passing through the village of Sinnington, however, he had a rather unfortunate accident. One of the wheels of the trap caught on some object at the side of the road, causing it to become dislodged from the axle. At the same time, the horse pulling the trap bolted, and the net result was that Cooper was launched from the trap in the style of a catapult. Unfortunately, he struck the road head first and never regained consciousness, dying very shortly after.

16 SEPTEMBER 1812 According to William Scott of Tadcaster, on this night he was at a public house on the highway between that town and York and had drunk ten and a half pints of ale, something which may have some reflection on the subsequent story. On his way home he was accompanied by a man named Thompson but, after that man left him, Richard Longthorn came up to him and demanded that he give him a guinea note he was carrying. When Scott refused, Longthorn was joined by another man named Steel and they threatened him with violence. Finally, as they reached a quarry, Thomas England appeared, carrying a cavalier's sword, and told him he would run him through. Scott then escaped the men, jumped over a hedge and managed to hide himself. The three men were tried and would have been executed if found guilty; however, all three testified that they had not seen or spoken to Scott on the night in question, and two had solid alibis. Meanwhile Thompson testified that he had remained walking with Scott until well after the quarry in question. It seems strange that these three men were put on trial for their lives for what, essentially, was probably no more than the rambling story of a drunk.

17 SEPTEMBER 1732 Rievaulx Abbey was among those left in ruins by Henry VIII during the Dissolution of the Monasteries. Henry gave the land to the Earl of Rutland, and from there it passed into the hands of the Duncombe family, who set about beautifying the property. On this date, some workmen were busy on the project when high winds caused a collapse of masonry from one of the towers; two workmen found themselves trapped underneath, and died from their injuries shortly afterwards.

Rievaulx Abbey. (Author's collection)

18 SEPTEMBER 1885 Interesting scenes occurred at an inquest in York into the death of a man named John Fields, who had died six days earlier. The inquest had been opened on the day of his death, at which his wife, Sarah Ann Fields, testified that he had been feeling ill that morning in their home in Albert Street, and that she had sent for the doctor but, by the time of his arrival, her husband was dead. At that time the coroner requested a post-mortem examination and adjourned the inquest. When it reopened on this date, the medical examiners confirmed that the man had died of natural causes. However, evidence was then taken from Anastasia Phelan of Middlesborough. The date of the Fields' marriage had been given as April the previous year, but Phelan stated that in March 1884 her husband had informed her that he had a new position with the Pearl Life Insurance Company in Sunderland and would send for her once he was settled. This was the last she saw of him. Producing a photograph, with his name given as John Phelan in his own handwriting, it was unmistakably the same man. Sarah, recalled to testify, stated that she had always known him as John Fields, had met him in Middlesborough, and was aware that he had lived in the same house as Mrs Phelan but was not aware that they had been married, and that he had always referred to her as a Mrs Kelly.

19 SEPTEMBER 1069 Over the course of the years 1068 and 1069, York changed hands several times between the forces of William the Conqueror and those of Edgar Aetheling, supported by the Scots and the Viking kingdoms. In response, William built two castles: the first in 1068 between the rivers Ouse and Foss, and the second in 1069 at Baile Hill on the west bank of the Ouse. On this date, a Danish

Statue of William the Conqueror from the choir screen of the minster. (Author's collection)

fleet supporting Aetheling sailed up the Ouse under the command of King Sweyn Estrithson of Denmark and attacked both castles, with the aid of the forces of Gospatrick, Earl of Northumbria. In response, the Norman forces defending the city set fire to some of the city houses in an attempt to hold the rebels back. The fire grew out of control, sweeping across the town and burning the minster to the ground as well as destroying at least one of the castles. William of Malet, leader of the Norman forces and Sheriff of York, was taken captive along with his wife and children and held hostage for the safety of the Viking forces. It was in response to this attack that William ordered the Harrying of the North, which is discussed elsewhere in this book.

20 SEPTEMBER 1319 One of the most memorable scenes in the movie *Braveheart* is that of the sacking of York. However, this is a fiction, made up by the scriptwriters and probably inspired by an event that took place on this date, some fourteen years after William Wallace's death. Having defeated the English at the Battle of Bannockburn five years earlier, Robert the Bruce was now making incursions into English territory, and an army led by the Earl of Moray and the Black Douglas had

Battlefield marker at Myton-on-Swale. (Author's collection)

entered Yorkshire and was approaching the city, their aim being to kidnap Queen Isabella, who was then in residence there. William de Melton, Archbishop of York, arranged for her to be taken to safety and then raised an army of 10,000 men from the city and its surrounds. Most of the men were not professional soldiers; many were armed with little more than pitchforks, and the fighting force included clergymen still dressed in their church vestments. They met the Scottish army at Myton-on-Swale, 10 miles north of the city, where – unsurprisingly – they were entirely massacred by the battle-hardened Scottish troops. Among the thousands of dead was Sir Nicholas Fleming, the only Lord Mayor of York to be killed in battle while in office.

21 **SEPTEMBER 1549** In the turmoil that followed the death of Henry VIII and during the regency of the Duke of Somerset, a number of armed revolts broke out in England, many fuelled by John Dudley, the Earl of Warwick, who wanted the regency for himself. Among these was the Seamer Rebellion in North Yorkshire, led by William Ombler. It began with the lighting of a beacon in Staxton, near Scarborough, and the crowds prepared to march on York, gathering support in villages along the way. Six people were killed by the rebels, including Matthew White, a chantry commissioner of York, and his brother. Contemporary reports speak of the rebels leaving their bodies 'naked behynde them in the playne fieldes for crowes to feede on'. The Council of the North sent out a force against them while also offering a free pardon to any who went peacefully back to their homes, and the rebellion began to peter out. Ombler was apprehended and executed at the Knavesmire in York on this date, together with seven other leaders of the revolt.

Statue of William de Melton, Archbishop of York, who led a ragtag army of priests and locals into battle against the Scots at Myton-on-Swale in 1319. (Author's collection)

22 SEPTEMBER 1946 After a lengthy hunt starting the previous evening, an 11-year-old boy found the body of 4-year-old Norma Dale on some wasteland in the Tang Hall district of the city. She had last been seen at 2.40 p.m. the previous day when she had come into her house from playing. Her mother had given her a rice cake, and she had gone out again. When she didn't return, her mother grew more and more concerned, and eventually a search party was organised to comb the district. The rate of ingestion of the rice cake showed she had probably been murdered within twenty minutes of the time she had last been seen. She had been strangled but there was no sign of sexual assault. Her mother stated, forty years on, that she believed a local woman had done it when young Norma had stumbled on her having an extramarital affair. However, a year later another young girl, 10-year-old Sheila Gowrie, was murdered in Manchester and there were several similarities: both girls were found on wasteland near their homes, both were strangled with no apparent motive, and both had their right shoe missing. Neither murder was ever solved, so it is still not known if the same person was responsible for both.

23 SEPTEMBER 1805 Elizabeth Stockden had been in service with a Mr Scholefield at Temple Newsome near Leeds for about nine years and had been left in charge of the house where only Thomas Atkinson, a steward to Viscountess Irwin, was staying. When she got up at 6 a.m. on this day, she approached the kitchen but encountered Atkinson with a crazed look in his eye, brandishing a hammer. He immediately attacked her, striking her several times with the claw end of the hammer before she managed to escape and secure herself in the kitchen. Atkinson ran outside and encountered another young girl, whom he informed that 'Lizzie is dead' and entreated her to take him to Mr Scholefield, but at that point Stockden emerged from the front door, screaming for help. Atkinson made to attack her again but she managed to secure herself inside the house, at which point he absconded and was discovered some weeks later in Hull after an advertisement had been posted in newspapers giving his description. He was tried at York and, after some technicality over the weapon, was executed at the Knavesmire on 6 May of the following year. Atkinson was just 15 years old at the time of his execution.

24 SEPTEMBER 1664 A deposition given at York Castle on this day accused a gentleman named Lionel Copley, Esq. of having 'beaten Richard Frith, put a bridle in his mouth, got on his back, and ridden him about for half an hour, kicking him to make him move'. There is no record of whether the matter was taken further, but Copley was a man of good standing, and indeed his son later went on to be Governor of Maryland.

25 SEPTEMBER 1066 Tostig Godwinson had been exiled a year earlier in events described in the entry for 3 October. Having travelled to Norway, he had made a pact with King Harald Hardrada to support his claim on the throne based on his being the heir of Cnut, who had been crowned English king some fifty years earlier. Along with an army of Scottish mercenaries, the two men had captured York at the Battle of Gate Fulford around five days before, and so King Harold – Tostig's brother – had raced north with a fully mounted army. On this date, the two armies clashed at Stamford Bridge, around 8 miles east of York. The speed with which Harold arrived took Tostig and Hardrada by surprise and they deployed their army quickly in a defensive circle east of the River Derwent. Legend has it that a giant Norseman defended the bridge, and had slaughtered forty English soldiers single-handedly before a man was sent down river in a barrel and thrust a spear into him through the slats of the bridge. This story is probably apocryphal but the bottleneck of the bridge certainly delayed the English army long enough to allow the Norse to set up a shield wall. However, they had not had time to fully don their armour and this was the deciding factor in the battle, which lasted several hours but eventually resulted in victory for Harold. Both Tostig and Hardrada were killed during the battle, and Norse casualties were said to be so heavy that of the 300 ships in which they had arrived, only twenty-four were required to take them home. Harold's casualties were also severe, with some estimates stating that over a third of his army were killed. Three days later, William of Normandy took advantage of this situation and invaded the

Tostig Godwinson and Harald Hardrada arrive in York, from *The Life of St Edward the Confessor* by Matthew Paris. (Author's collection)

Monument and plaque marking the location of the Battle of Stamford Bridge. (Author's collection)

South Coast of England, so that it was a battle-weary and depleted force that Harold then had to rush southwards to meet the invaders at Hastings.

26 SEPTEMBER 1799 Thomas Hodgson was highly superstitious and often consulted with three associates he referred to as 'cunning men'. Hodgson had been robbed of the sum of £135 earlier in the year, and while he was sure that his former employee Michael Simpson was the culprit, and was attempting to prove such, he received in the post three pills, purporting to be from the 'cunning men'. Accompanying them was a note informing him that if he took them at 9 p.m. and lay on his left side, then rose from his bed at 1 a.m. on this date, when he looked out of his window he would see the face of the man who had stolen the money. Unfortunately this was not the case, as the pills turned out to be poison; almost immediately, Hodgson began experiencing stomach pains, and his wife forced melted

butter down his throat to make him vomit the pills back up. However, it was to no avail and he died from their effects. The pills were traced back to Simpson, who claimed he had been given them by a 'wise man'; he claimed to be unaware of the effect they would have, saying that he was just trying to help his former employer. However, he was not believed, and he was hanged for Hodgson's murder in March of the following year.

27 SEPTEMBER 1861 Until the nineteenth century the Ouse Bridge was the only road crossing of the river in the city, but in 1838 a suggestion was put forward to replace the ferry service, which operated between Barker Tower and Lendal Tower, with a second bridge. The foundation stone was laid in October 1860 on a latticed girder bridge, and work moved swiftly until this date when, with the bridge nearing completion, disaster struck. As workmen attempted to raise a girder using hydraulics, it became unmanageable and canted over, falling into the latticework of the bridge which was said to have wobbled for a moment before appearing to remain sturdy, but then began to collapse like a house of cards. As it did, one of the girders on the south side crashed into the gantry where workmen were engaged in riveting work, and several men were swept 50ft into the waters below. Some were rescued in boats and others swam to safety, but three were swept away and drowned, including 10-year-old Thomas Hoyle. Of the fifty men working on the bridge at the time of the collapse, it was said that very few escaped with no injury at all. A youth named John Masser was struck by a falling girder and killed instantly. Another man, John Manuel, was trapped under a fallen girder, which was said to have nearly cut him in half. He was still alive when discovered, but it took half an hour to remove the girder from his body, by which time he had expired.

28 SEPTEMBER 1896 William Ward, a confectioner living in Winterscale Street, off Fishergate, had fallen on hard times. A widower with no children, he had set himself up in business as a result of an inheritance, but business was no longer going well and he had recently had to sell some of his furniture to make ends meet. On this date he borrowed sixpence from a neighbour, Mrs Rispin, and then used the money in two chemist shops, one in Fulford Road and the other in High Ousegate, these being sufficiently distant that he clearly did not want anyone to know what he was doing. In both shops he bought a quantity of laudanum, claiming that he wished to calm stomach cramps. He then returned home, swallowed both draughts and retired to bed, leaving a note for Mrs Rispin apologising that he would be unable to repay her kindness. He was found dead the following day after failing to open his shop.

29 SEPTEMBER 1469 The execution of Sir Humphrey Neville in York on this date is an example of how no good deed goes unpunished. Sir Humphrey was a cousin to Richard Neville, the Earl of Warwick (known as the Kingmaker), and while Warwick had chosen the Yorkist side in the Wars of the Roses, Sir Humphrey was a staunch Lancastrian. After the Lancaster defeat at the Battle of Hexham, Sir Humphrey went into hiding in the Scottish border country, from where he continued to agitate for the Lancaster cause. He returned to aid his cousin's capture of King Edward IV, whereby Warwick – along with Edward's brother George Plantagenet – attempted to rule through their control over the king. But Warwick was not content with this and, wanting Henry VI returned to the throne, he launched an uprising that Edward was forced to put down. However, Edward was captured during the battle and imprisoned by Warwick for three months. Unfortunately for Warwick, the other nobles would not lend their armies to the cause as long as the king was captured, and so he was forced to release Edward. Hence, when Edward had Neville publicly beheaded on this date, he was effectively executing Sir Humphrey for returning him to power.

30 SEPTEMBER 1594 Edward Osbaldston was born in Lancashire, near Blackburn, and as a young man travelled to France, where he was ordained as a priest, leading his first Mass on the feast day of St Jerome in 1585. Exactly nine years later, on this date, he was arrested while staying at an inn in Tollerton, after a former Catholic priest named Thomas Clark, who had converted to the Protestant faith and with whom Osbaldston had preached in the past, recognised him and informed the authorities. He was taken to York Castle and, as with so many other Catholic priests, sentenced to death. While awaiting his execution in the castle he wrote a letter to fellow priest Father Richard Holtby, describing the events of his arrest. In the letter he expressed forgiveness for Clark, asking that God grant him the courage to face death as bravely as his fellow martyrs. He was executed on 16 November.

OCTOBER

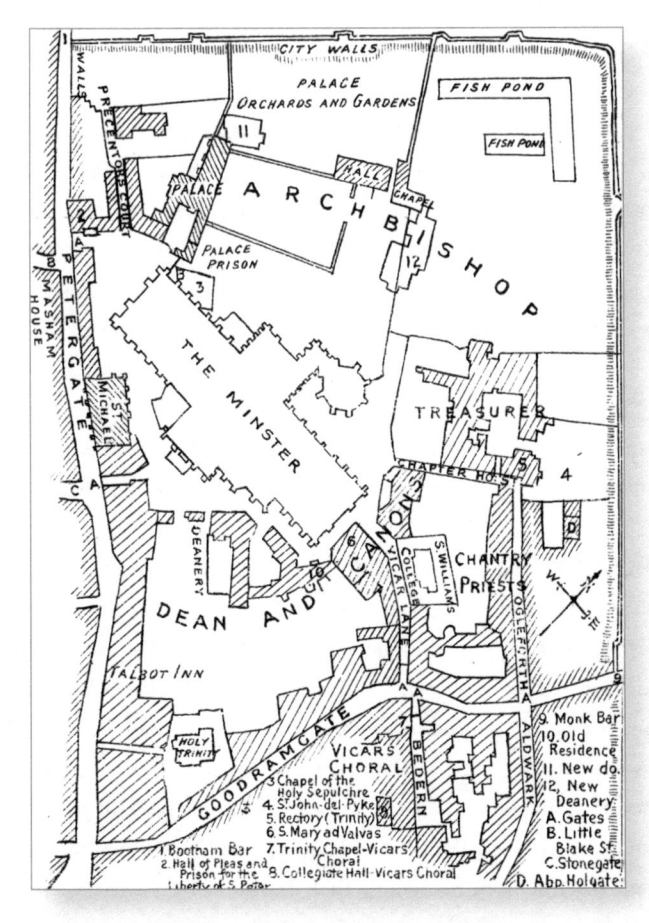

Map showing the layout of the minster and its surrounding buildings in the eighteenth century. (Author's collection)

1 OCTOBER 1770 Michael Naylor was executed at the Knavesmire on this date for the murder of a man named William Lund. He had been tried at the August assizes in York and his execution date was set for 23 August, but the confirmation of that order had been held up and had not arrived in time. It was finally received in the last week of September and his delayed execution was hastily arranged. Naylor had been employed as a mower, and had stabbed Lund in the stomach with his scythe when the other man apparently slighted him by asking if he 'still rose so early in the morning', a suggestion that he was up to no good. A second man who had rushed to Lund's aid had also been stabbed with a chisel but recovered from the injury, and Naylor had also attacked the landlady of the public house where the incident took place, but when he attempted to stab her, her stays deflected the blow.

2 OCTOBER 1899 John Dunn, a 56-year-old joiner living in Alma Terrace, informed his wife that he was going to Fulford to see a dog. On his return, at around 10.45 p.m., he had a lump on his head the size of an egg, and was barely able to speak. He went to bed and the following morning – his condition not having improved – a doctor was sent for, who examined him and declared him unlikely to recover. By now Dunn had lapsed into a coma, and he died later that day. It transpired that Dunn had not gone to Fulford, but to the house of some neighbours in the same street where he had spent time with a Mrs Latham, whose husband was convinced that the two were conducting an affair and had warned Dunn to stay away. At some point during the evening, Norman Latham had returned home and found Dunn with his wife, and the two men had ended up fighting in the backyard, where a neighbour saw Latham swing something, probably a broom, and strike Dunn in the head.

3 OCTOBER 1065 Tostig Godwinson had been appointed Earl of Northumbria in 1055, but was never a popular leader. Preferring to spend his time in the south, and rarely visiting York, when he was present he generally treated the local nobles with disdain and often resorted to assassination to achieve his aims. On this date, it seems the people had taken all they could of his rule. The *Anglo-Saxon Chronicle* tells us that 'all the thanes in Yorkshire and in Northumberland gathered themselves together at York, and outlawed their Earl Tostig, slaying all the men of his clan that they could reach, both Danish and English, and took all his weapons in York, with gold and silver, and all his money that they could anywhere there find'. Declaring Morcar, the younger brother of the Earl of Mercia, as their new earl, they marched south and demanded that King Edward the Confessor confirm this change. Edward sent Harold Godwinson to negotiate and, seeing no alternative, he agreed to have his

brother outlawed and exiled. It was a decision he may have come to regret a year later on his defeat at the Battle of Hastings (see entry for 25 September).

4 OCTOBER 1748 Church Fenton is a small village around 10 miles to the south of York, and on this date, one of its residents, Robert Fawthorpe, celebrated his wedding. The previous day the village had been shocked by a bloody crime that took place in its midst. Elizabeth Ferrand and Mary Parker ran a small grocery store in the village, and some of the villagers were attracted to the place by the barking of a dog. Finding it locked up in the middle of the day, they broke in and found the bloodied corpses of the two women, who had apparently been attacked with a cooper's adze. The shop and house attached had been robbed of all its money and valuables. Two days after Fawthorpe's wedding he was arrested for the crime, having apparently been trying to set himself up with enough money to settle down to married life. Fawthorpe was tried at the York Assizes, and executed at the Knavesmire the following March.

5 OCTOBER 1568 On 10 February 1567, Lord Darnley, husband of Mary, Queen of Scots, was murdered at Kirk o' Fields in Edinburgh. Just three months later, Mary married the Earl of Bothwell. He was suspected of being Darnley's killer, at Mary's behest in revenge for Darnley's killing of her royal favourite, David Rizzio. The Scottish nobles objected to this marriage, imprisoned Mary at Lochleven Castle and forced her abdication. However, she escaped and threw herself on the mercy of her cousin, the English Queen Elizabeth. Elizabeth convened a conference to be held in York to discuss whether or not Mary should be charged with Darnley's murder. On this date, Earl Moray, ruling Scotland as regent to Mary's infant son James, produced a series of documents at that conference purporting to be eight letters and some sonnets written in Mary's handwriting and addressed to Bothwell, proving her complicity in the murder. These are now known as the Casket Letters. Mary claimed the letters to be forgeries, and their authenticity has been hotly debated ever since. Elizabeth engineered the conference so that it would neither confirm Mary's guilt nor exonerate her, in order to give her legitimacy to hold Mary prisoner without trying her for any crime.

6 OCTOBER 1886 A report appears in several newspapers of this date of a young 20-year-old singer from York named Julia Hewitt, who was performing at a concert in Malton. During the course of her performance, she is said to have suddenly thrown her arms in the air, groaned, and collapsed to the stage. Audience members who rushed to her aid quickly discovered that the girl had died. At her inquest, the verdict given was 'death from syncope, by a visitation of God'.

7 OCTOBER

1817 Thomas Riley, a prisoner at the castle, was awaiting his trial for high treason. Riley was considered not to be of particularly sound mind, on account of the fact that he had twice attempted to commit suicide by hanging himself in his cell: the first time in Huddersfield before being transferred to the castle prison, and the second after his arrival. At about 4 a.m. on this date, in a bed he was sharing with four other men, he cut his own throat using a razor he had managed to procure from one of the other prisoners. On this occasion his attempt was successful and he died just minutes later.

8 OCTOBER

1586 Robert Bickerdyke was from Knaresborough, but was in York for the execution of the Catholic priest Francis Ingleby. As part of the punishment, Ingleby was to be dragged to his place of execution tied to a hurdle. As he passed through the streets, Bickerdyke heard a lady say to her sister, 'let us go to the Tollbooth, and we shall see the traitorly thief come over on the hurdle'. Unable to stay his tongue, Bickerdyke turned to her and replied 'no, no thief, as true as thou art'. This laid suspicion that he, too, was of the Catholic faith. He was later arrested for giving aid to a priest, John Boste, by giving him a glass of ale to quench his thirst. At his trial, the two ladies he had addressed, one of whom turned out to be the wife of a Protestant minister, gave evidence against him. He was initially acquitted, but tried a second time and found guilty. He was executed on this date.

9 OCTOBER

1771 William Moore was an elderly man from Alne who went about the countryside of North Yorkshire selling oatmeal. On this night he was in Sheriff Hutton, in the company of a man named John Lazenby, and set out at around 11 p.m. to return home. During the night he had proposed a wager with Lazenby, which the other man had not accepted, but Moore had shown him the money he had about his person to prove that he was good for the bet. Lazenby determined to get his hands on the money and so followed Moore after he had left the drinking establishment. When they were a suitable distance away, Lazenby attacked Moore with a fencepost, striking him several times around the head. Moore passed away and his body was discovered the following morning. Lazenby initially attempted to implicate another man, but eventually confessed and was executed the following year.

10 OCTOBER

1820 The death of a rather singular man by the name of Lumley Kettlewell, living in the Pavement in York, occurred on or around this date. He was said to have been a gentleman of good manners and breeding, but had retired from the world to become a hermit. He lived in a house that he had barricaded up so no one might enter, and he himself came and went by climbing a ladder and squeezing through a small window. Inside, he shared the property with a menagerie of animals, including dogs, ducks, a fox, and a large brown ass, and rats were said to roam freely. He owned horses that regularly died due to his forgetting to feed them. The house was said to be squalid, filthy and unheated, and he slept in a wooden crate filled with hay. He is said to have drunk only vinegar and water, and dined on strange concoctions of food such as cock's heads cooked in a pudding of bran and treacle. Notwithstanding his unusual lifestyle, he was apparently in his seventies at the time of his death.

11   OCTOBER 1883   Three men were working at the railway works in York, constructing a pit in a new workshop, when a pile of bricks next to the hole in which they were working became unstable and fell into the hole on top of them. Workers quickly tried to clear away the bricks and pull the men out, but one of them, named Patrick Quinn, had already been crushed to death. The other two men survived the accident, although one was rushed to the hospital where his back was found to have been broken.

12   OCTOBER 1899   Rose Hannah Dickson, 14, had lost her mother the previous Christmas, and on this morning she had apparently had some sort of argument with her father at their home in Poppleton Road. After her father went out to work, she went to the house of a neighbour, Martha Hodman, and asked for an envelope. Returning home, she left again at around 1 p.m. and walked to the water works. There she encountered a 10-year-old boy named Ernest Cleveland, whom she handed a letter and then promptly jumped into the river. Her body was recovered later that day. The boy gave the letter to his mother who – although it was addressed to the girl's sister in Oldham – opened it. Inside the girl had written, 'I am very sorry to tell you that my father was calling me this morning. He said he could do better without me than with me, so I am going to try it on. By the time you get this, I shall be drowned.' She also included a Christmas card.

13   OCTOBER 1891   York was struck on this day by winds said to have been of hurricane strength, which caused great damage to property throughout the city. John Pinkney, a 13-year-old boy living with his father at Barbican Road, was crossing St George's Field where Clarke's Circus had set up and as he passed, a corrugated-iron

roof from one of the temporary structures was ripped from its mounting by the wind and struck him end on in the side of the head. It caused such severe fracturing of his skull that he never regained consciousness and died within a few hours.

14 OCTOBER 1322 King Edward II arrived in York on this day in rather unusual circumstances. Since the beginning of the year, the Scots – emboldened by the near civil war that had been happening in England between Edward and his nobles – had been making regular raids across the border to try to force Edward to begin peace negotiations and recognise Robert the Bruce as the rightful Scottish king. In revenge, Edward had made a raid into Scotland, reaching Edinburgh before being beaten back across the border. He was recuperating at Rievaulx Abbey on his way back to London when Bruce crossed the border and moved his army south at rapid speed, reaching Northallerton on the 13th and setting the town on fire. On this date, Edward was at dinner with the abbot when Bruce's army approached, and as a result the king was forced to leave his meal half-eaten, fleeing into the safety of York's city walls while his army attempted to halt the Scottish approach. Unfortunately, they were routed and many of them put to the sword.

15 OCTOBER 1875 An affray between gamekeepers and poachers occurred on this day on an estate north of York. John Goodwill, the son of a farmer on the estate, was ferreting for rabbits in the company of another man named Carswell when John Harrison, the gamekeeper, spotted them and told them to stop. As Harrison headed home, he was apprehended by other members of the Goodwill family and a man named Smith, who broke his gun and threatened him with violence. To settle the matter, it was decided that Smith and Harrison would fight, and they proceeded to go a few rounds with each other, during which time Harrison's son, Holmes Harrison, came upon the scene. As he looked on, John Goodwill came up behind him and struck him about the head with a hedge stake and, knocking him to the ground, beat him several more times so that those present thought he must be dead. In fact he survived, but suffered a fractured skull and was paralysed by the attack. Goodwill was found guilty of causing grievous bodily harm, and sentenced to six months' hard labour.

16 OCTOBER 1884 A bizarre case put before the police court was reported in the *York Herald* for this date. According to the story, Sergeant Darley of the York Police was patrolling in Heworth Road when a man named John Walker came up to him and informed him that two young boys wished to give him into custody. The policeman could see no boys, so tried to get some sense out of the man, who would only say that he had

knocked one of the boys down. Suddenly, the two boys came running down the street, at which point Walker stepped behind the policeman. One of these boys, 13-year-old Joseph Cockerill, informed Darley that a man had knocked him down and that he was sure he could identify him. At this point, Walker stepped out from behind the sergeant and said 'I am sure too', and punched the boy in the face so hard that his feet left the ground.

17 OCTOBER 1917 Harry Barker, a 28-year-old man working as a cashier at the York School for the Blind, had decided that he wished to join the war effort and enlisted in the army. He and his wife lived in the village of Elvington, just on the outskirts of the city, and had made arrangements that she would stay there while he was away. He was said to be very keen to serve his country; however, it was said that she was becoming ever more depressed, convinced that she would never see her husband again once he left. The couple kept a number of fowl, and on this date – the day before his intended departure – neighbours noticed that nobody had fed them that day, and that the couple had not been seen. They tried the door but, getting no answer, forced their way in and found the couple in their night attire with their throats cut. From the evidence it appeared that Barker had first killed his wife, and then committed suicide.

18 OCTOBER 1780 William Meyer had not long been married when he fell into arrears on the house he had rented for his wife and himself, and as a result received a visit from the sheriff's officer. Meyer was not home at the time, and his wife advised the bailiff to obtain money from Meyer's mother, who lived in Kirk Hammerton, some few miles outside of York. He agreed to ride there and left an assistant, John Spink, to guard the house in the meantime. Shortly afterwards, Meyer returned home and demanded that Spink leave his property, but he had his orders and refused to do so. At this point Meyer told his wife to fetch his pistols, which were already loaded. On having them placed in his hands, he raised one and shot Spink in the neck, severing his carotid artery and causing him to bleed to death in a matter of minutes. He was executed the following year, the cart from York Castle to the Knavesmire passing by the very house in which the murder had taken place. His wife stood trial alongside him, but was acquitted.

19 OCTOBER 1804 On this date, a man entered the shop of William Perkin, a druggist, and asked for a quantity of laudanum for his father who, he stated, was troubled with pain that kept him awake at night. The man gave his name as Joseph Fletcher, and was given a little over an ounce of the drug. A few days later, a pair of sisters, Elizabeth and Sarah Fletcher, became insensible after drinking some ale given them by their lodger Joseph Brown, which he had sweetened with sugar. Sarah went into

a deep sleep from which she did not wake until late the following day, while Elizabeth went into convulsions and died. By the time an investigation showed that the sisters had been poisoned, Brown and his fellow lodger Joseph Hazelgrove, had absconded. Four years later, Brown entered a police office on the Isle of Wight and made a full confession, stating that he and Hazelgrove had set out only to murder Elizabeth, in order to steal the contents of a box she kept, although when they opened the box it contained only a guinea and a half. He also confessed to an earlier murder, stating that these events were playing on his mind such that he could get no peace until he confessed. Brown and Hazelgrove had also been tried and found guilty of a theft from a granary some years earlier, and had been sentenced to death, but their sentences had been commuted on condition they joined the army. At trial Brown was found guilty as charged and was hanged in 1809, but the charges against Hazelgrove were dropped.

20 OCTOBER 1663 Reports emerged of a strange case of a man who got himself into what could have been serious trouble. A father and son, both called Richard Readshaw, had been accused of stealing money from Lord Fairfax, and were now held in York Gaol. A visiting friend informed them that he knew of a man named Nicholas Battersby who was skilled in the art of divining where stolen money might be. He came to see the Readshaws, and after asking some questions went away and returned the next day, informing the local sheriff that the money was stolen by two servants of Lord Fairfax, an old grey-haired man and a young man, and that it was hidden in a sack and would be found again in five months' time. The sheriff accepted this information, but realising that it could only have been obtained through witchcraft, arrested Battersby accordingly. Luckily for him, having caused no harm to anybody, at his trial he was bound over for good behaviour.

21 OCTOBER 1536 Following the Dissolution of the Monasteries by Henry VIII, there was considerable unrest in the North, and on 2 October an uprising had broken out in Lincolnshire, protesting the formation of the Church of England. This was put down, but a second uprising broke out on 13 October in Yorkshire, coining for itself the name the Pilgrimage of Grace. A London barrister named Robert Aske, who hailed from Aughton near Selby, was asked to lead the movement, and on this date he led a band of somewhere between 9,000 and 10,000 men into York, driving out the new tenants of the buildings Henry had sold off in the Dissolution and returning them to their previous monastic occupants, as well as ordering the return of Catholic observance in the churches and the minster. The occupation of the city lasted until 27 October, when Henry sent his aide Thomas Howard, the Duke of Norfolk, to negotiate with the rebels,

who by now were said to number around 35,000. Howard promised a pardon to all involved and a parliament to be held in York within a year to negotiate a compromise; Aske agreed to the terms and dismissed his followers. This would turn out to be a mistake, as within a year, Aske would be executed for treason.

22 OCTOBER 1884 Albert Robinson, the ostler for the Black Swan Hotel in Coney Street, was returning there at about 6.30 p.m. According to witnesses at the time, he was travelling at somewhere between 12 and 14mph, which was considered a reckless pace for such a busy street. As the cart came to the clock at St Martin's church, John Copeland, who was riding on the cart, saw two boys in the street dividing up newspapers between them. He shouted to the boys, who he believed were about 10 yards away at the time, and they jumped each to a different side of the road. One of the boys struck the wheel on the offside of the cart and was thrown to the pavement. The injured boy, 13-year-old Thomas Rooney, was rushed to hospital, where he died an hour after admission. Although those on the cart claimed the boy was simply struck by the wheel, the house surgeon at the hospital was of the opinion that his injuries – a fractured skull and several broken ribs – could only have been caused by the cartwheel actually running him over. Robinson was indicted for reckless driving, but the case was rejected by the grand jury.

Coney Street in the early twentieth century. (Author's collection)

23 OCTOBER 1930 Evelyn Jefferson, in service to the Halder family of Burton Lane in York, was last seen alive on this evening by her friend Muriel Wilson, whom she told about a letter she had received from a young man she had met. The family had gone away for a few days and returned on the Saturday morning to find the house full of gas from the cooker, and Evelyn laying dead on the floor. She had left a note, stating that her heart was broken by the death of her sister some months earlier, and saying, 'bury me beside Mabel and we two girls will then be together'. The incident is a sequel to the story related in this book for 10 June, when Mabel had been the victim of a suicide pact in the village of Bishop Wilton.

24 OCTOBER 1821 Two workmen, William Thompson and Robert Coleman, had been contracted to perform some work in the cellar of the Cross Keys public house in Goodramgate on this date, and had dug down around 2.5ft below the surface when they came across a human skeleton. From the state of body, it was estimated that the burial had taken place not more than ten years earlier, as there was still some decomposed flesh clinging to the bones. Mr Turner, the landlord of the establishment, professed no knowledge of how the body had come to be there, or when it had been deposited. He had not been the publican ten years previously and was sure that it had not been buried there during his occupancy. The matter remains a mystery.

25 OCTOBER 1675 Bull baiting is today considered an example of one of the barbarous sports carried out during the Middle Ages. The bull was tied to a stake, and dogs would then dart at the bull from various directions and attempt to bite it. Sometimes the bull got its own back; in 1611 there was a report of a bull breaking free while being baited in Easingwold, and goring three of the spectators to death. Usually pepper was blown up the bull's nose prior to the event in order to enrage it and make the spectacle more entertaining. However, these entertainments were also considered to have a practical purpose, as the meat of the animal was claimed to taste better if the bull had been baited before slaughter. As such, laws had been passed stating that this had to be done, and this law was not actually rescinded until 1835. On this date, a butcher named Robert Hardin was apparently fined 2*s* for selling meat from bulls that had not been baited.

26 OCTOBER 1897 During an argument at the house where he lodged with his uncle, Herbert Hansell lost his temper and threw a lighted lamp at his fellow lodger, Thomas Newham. The paraffin from the lamp poured on to the man and ignited, causing him severe burns from which he soon after died. Hansell was found guilty of manslaughter and sentenced to five years in prison.

27 OCTOBER 1679 Robert Bolron was a native of Newcastle-upon-Tyne who, on returning from fighting in the Dutch Wars, visited an old acquaintance who was a servant at Barnbow Hall in Yorkshire, and while there was offered a position managing the collieries of Sir Thomas Gascoigne. He married a servant there, Mary Baker, and settled in a farm at Shippon Hall. On this date he appeared at York Castle before the Lord Mayor to make some startling accusations against his employer: that he was a recusant of the Catholic faith and was involved in a Popish plot to assassinate King Charles II, which he had attempted to bribe Bolron into joining. The accusation was considered so serious that Sir Thomas was taken to trial on Bolron's evidence, backed up with that of another servant, Laurence Marbury, and if found guilty, he would certainly have lost his life. However, at trial it transpired that Marbury had recently been discharged by his master for theft, and that Bolron had been threatened by Gascoigne's daughter with prosecution for embezzling her father's money. Sir Thomas, who was 85 years old at the time, was found not guilty of the charges. Bolron gave evidence against several others for Catholic activities and a year later one Thomas Thweng of Heworth in York was executed for conducting services in the garments of a Catholic priest on his testimony. Thweng was initially given a stay on account of Bolron's unreliability, but eventually the Privy Council decided that the execution should go ahead.

28 OCTOBER 1940 York was under a 'purple' air-raid warning, meaning that enemy aircraft were expected to fly overhead but not attack. So far York had only suffered one bombing since the outbreak of war, and this had caused some damage of property but no fatalities. On this night, that was to change. Four small-calibre bombs were released over the Elmfield Avenue area of the city, the first one landing on open ground and the second destroying a barn. However, the third bomb landed in the front garden of No. 11 Sefton Gardens, just as two air-raid wardens – both of whom lived in the street – were in the vicinity. John March, 34, was nearest to the explosion and was said to have taken the full force of it and died instantly. His colleague Henry Coles also received a fatal chest wound and died very quickly. Property was said to have been damaged for 100 yards on either side of the explosion. The fourth bomb dropped harmlessly.

29 OCTOBER 1892 Throughout its history, York has been a city prone to flooding. On this date, the *York Herald* reported on damage caused during nearly two weeks of constant floods within the city, particularly in the Walmgate area. The chief

cause of disaster was that men were digging new sewers for the street, and had been digging a tunnel from two different ends, which was about 6ft away from meeting up in the middle. When the floodwaters came rushing in, they not only swept away that middle section, but also they scoured the walls and caused a considerable widening of the tunnel as brickwork had not yet been added. Then, once the water had receded, the ground above became unstable, and buildings started to subside. Thankfully no life was lost, but several buildings collapsed and businesses had to close down due to the loss of their warehouses.

30 OCTOBER 1850 At around 3 a.m., fire engines were called to the scene of one of the largest fires the city has seen. The scene of the fire – which had broken out unnoticed at around 10.30 p.m. the previous day – was Cattley's sawmill in Skeldergate, where there was a vast quantity of wood in stock. Furthermore, a recent delivery had stacked some 30 tons of coal against the back wall of the premises. By the time the engines arrived, the roof of the building had collapsed, and the flames were said to be so high in the night sky as to make the surrounding area as light as day. So fierce was it that on arrival the firemen realised that there was no chance of tackling the blaze and instead directed their efforts at ensuring it did not spread to any of the neighbouring warehouses, while allowing it to burn itself out. Remarkably, there was no loss of life, not even of two horses that were trapped in the blaze and for which rescuers ran through the flames to cut their halters and allow them to flee.

31 OCTOBER 1454 The second Battle of Stamford Bridge was a much smaller affair than its illustrious predecessor of 1066, but was one of the major turning points in the feud between the Neville and Percy families, which preceded the Wars of the Roses. Since an attack by Thomas Percy, Lord Egremont, on a Neville wedding party on Heworth Moor the previous year, tensions had been running high between the families, and when a Neville party came upon Egremont riding with 200 retainers on Neville land, the two parties faced up to each other. The Neville force clearly being the stronger, many on the Percy side turned and fled, leaving Egremont and his younger brother Richard Percy defenceless; they were soon captured. Held under arrest, their fate was left in the hands of Richard, Duke of York, who was then acting as Lord Protector of the Realm, as King Henry VI's fragile mental state had collapsed the previous year. Richard naturally sided with his allies, the Nevilles, and Egremont was ordered to pay over £11,000 in damages, a sum far beyond his means. As a result, the brothers were committed to a debtors' prison, where they remained for two years before managing to escape.

NOVEMBER

Merchant's Hall, also known as the Merchant Adventurer's Hall. (Author's collection)

1 NOVEMBER 866 Two years before this date, the Viking leader Ragnar Lodbrok invaded Northumbria and was captured and executed by the Northumbrian king, Aelle, by being thrown into a pit of poisonous snakes. The sons of Ragnar swore vengeance and two of his younger sons, Ivar the Boneless and Halfdan Ragnarsson, raised a mighty invading army known as the Great Heathen Army. They arrived on the coast of Anglia, where the local king made peace and presented them with 1,000 horses, enabling them to ride to York and prepare to storm the city. Knowing that the city was a centre of Christian worship, they chose this date for their attack because it was All Saints Day, when every person of note would be in church. They swept through the city almost unopposed, putting all who would not yield to the sword and sacking the churches and houses. However, Aelle was not present, so they turned their attention northward and spent the winter in the region of the Tyne before returning to the city in even greater numbers the following March.

Recreated face of a Viking warrior from the skull of a member of the Great Heathen Army. (Author's collection)

2 NOVEMBER 1882 Three young boys were enjoying themselves in a boat in the River Foss, near to the Monk Bridge coal wharf, on this date. One of the three, Robert Cattley, son of a widow in the Monkgate, was stood up in the boat when he overbalanced and went over the side. His two companions, Arthur Rymer and William Turner, tried to bring the boat around in order to rescue him, but found themselves unable to do so. A man named Robert Musgrave, who was standing nearby, jumped into the river and waded out, but was unable to reach Cattley for some minutes. A policeman named Thornton came to help him and the two men finally managed to drag the boy from the water, but it was too late as he had already drowned. Cattley was said to be 12 years of age.

3 NOVEMBER 1640 Thomas Wentworth, the 1st Earl of Strafford, was a loyal supporter and close confidante of King Charles I during the years prior to the English Civil War. Hailing from the East Riding of Yorkshire, one of his many appointments under the king was as President of the Council of the North, which

met at the King's Manor in York. It was while in residence at this building on this date that Wentworth was summoned to London by the king. Charles had been forced to call a parliament whose first act was to call for the impeachment of Wentworth for high misdemeanours. Although Charles had promised he would 'not suffer in his person, honour or fortune', Parliament was determined to have Wentworth executed, and eventually the king had no choice but to sign his death warrant. Wentworth is said to have received the news with the words 'Put not your trust in Princes.' He was publicly beheaded on Tower Hill, and his execution is said to have been attended by the largest crowd seen in London up to that date.

4 NOVEMBER 1933 Alexander Nix, a fireman employed by the LNER railway company, was fixing an engine to a goods train at Challoner's Whin junction, about 2 miles from York, on this morning. It was about 6.30 a.m. and, having brought the engine to a standstill, he found he needed to alight in order to attend to a lamp. However, in the early morning gloom, he failed to spot an approaching passenger train, and as he made his way around the side of the train he stepped on to the track to one side and was almost immediately struck and killed.

5 NOVEMBER 1921 Roy Elliott was a chauffeur, working for Colonel Brian Fairfax of Middleham Manor. On this evening his employer asked to be driven to visit his brother, who lived at Bilbrough Hall, and on reaching the hall he was told to take the car to the garage. As he had driven the colonel to that location on many occasions, and was never required to drive him back again until at least 11 p.m., Elliott went into the village for a meal at the local inn. He was smoking a cigarette when he returned to get the car ready and found the colonel waiting in the garage. The colonel berated him for being late and, when Elliott tried to reply, the other man shouted, 'don't speak to me with that cigarette in your mouth' and knocked him to the ground, climbed on top of him and began to strangle him. Although Fairfax claimed he had acted in self-defence when the other man attacked him, the evidence of injury to Elliott's neck suggested otherwise. Fairfax was ordered to pay 20 guineas in damages to his former employee, and allow him to continue living in the cottage that had been part of his work arrangement.

6 NOVEMBER 1884 Annie Maud Brown was somewhat relieved on this date when the grand jury at the York Assizes concluded that there was not enough evidence to prosecute her on a charge of arson. A similar charge had already been dismissed against her husband, George Brown, after fire had destroyed a barn and all the property therein, belonging to George Lancaster at Knapton (then a small village just outside York, although now within the bounds of the city). A few days before the fire, Annie's son by a previous suitor had been sent to a reformatory school until his 16th birthday after being charged with damage to property by Lancaster, and the assumption – most likely correct – was that either one or both of the couple had started the fire in revenge. However, as neither one could be charged with the crime, there was no choice but to dismiss the case.

7 NOVEMBER 1896 After a manhunt lasting nearly two weeks, and conducted all across Yorkshire, a travelling hawker named John Winter – but known to locals across the county as Black Jack – was finally apprehended on this day. The length of the hunt was not due to Winter being on the run, but simply because he was unaware that he was wanted and had proven difficult to track down. In August of that year, Thomas Potter, who ran a sweet shop in Church Fenton, had complained to his daughter of suffering pains which, while not being debilitating, continued to trouble him until 2 October, when he was in such pain that a doctor was called to attend him. Although treatment was attempted, his condition continued to deteriorate and he died on 23 October. A post-mortem showed that the cause of death was a chronic gastric condition, which appeared to have been caused by violence. A young girl who lived next door remembered that around the time the illness began she had heard arguing in the shop, and had seen a fight in the shop between Potter and Black Jack in which the latter man had kicked him in the stomach three times, and she had fetched a man named Ambler, who dragged him away and threw him out of the house. Winter was found guilty of manslaughter, and sentenced to five years' hard labour.

8 NOVEMBER 1746 Following the defeat of the Jacobite rebellion at Culloden, the Duke of Cumberland rounded up all those known to have Jacobite sympathies and sent them for trial in England. Twenty-two were tried at York Assizes and sentenced to be hanged, drawn and quartered at the Knavesmire, and these executions were carried out in two tranches: ten on 1 November and the remaining twelve on this date. Each man was hanged, before his body was laid out and his heart removed and held aloft by the executioner with a cry of 'Gentlemen, behold the heart of a traitor!' Their heads were then removed, although the bodies were not actually quartered but merely scored on the arms and legs with a knife. Two heads were displayed on the Micklegate Bar, but the rest were buried with their bodies. The two heads were later stolen by a sympathiser named William Arundell, who is believed to have buried them in the churchyard of the Holy Trinity in Goodramgate.

9 NOVEMBER 1861 An inquest was held in York on this date into the death of Ann Abbey, an 80-year-old woman living in St Saviourgate with her daughter, Jane Bradley, a widow whose husband had committed suicide a year earlier. The inquest heard that the woman had treated her mother abominably, and had kept her a virtual prisoner. Recently the woman had tried to leave, leaning heavily on a stick, but had fallen and her daughter had dragged her back inside and beaten her mercilessly. It was suggested that this was the eventual cause of her death, and the coroner informed Bradley that he and the jury would visit her house to view her mother's body. On arrival, it was found that the house was locked and Bradley had gone away with the key. The door was consequently broken down, and inside the body was found to be in a very poor condition, covered in bruises around the arms and torso. However, there being some evidence that the woman was in the habit of falling, the jury at the inquest was unable to conclude whether Bradley had been responsible for her mother's death or not, but recommended the coroner censure her severely for her treatment of the woman.

10 NOVEMBER 1881 Having sunk a shaft to the depth of 22ft on a new gasworks at Foss Side, a workman named Thomas Moran was down in the shaft working on the fixing of pumping equipment when, without warning, he seems to have been overcome with fumes and fell to the bottom of the well. Two of his fellow workers, George Whiteley and Thomas Dalby, rushed to descend the shaft to check on their workmate, but as they descended to the level from which Moran had fallen, the same occurred and they too fell. In the meantime, a ladder had been lowered down the shaft and as soon as it was in place, James Clark began to climb down. On reaching the same depth, he fell also. Another man named Fox began to descend, but the foreman of the works pulled him back up again, realising that the danger was too great, and another man named Baxter also descended a distance without reaching the same depth. Eventually the four men were pulled out of the shaft using grappling irons, but three of the four were found to be dead, and Clark was barely breathing and expired shortly after. Fox and Baxter were also both found to be in serious respiratory distress, but later recovered. Experiments conducted by lowering lighted candles into the shaft, which immediately extinguished on reaching the depth in question, showed that an accumulation of toxic gasses had filled the lower portion.

11 NOVEMBER 1931 Alexander Morton was part of a demolition crew and was working on the top storey of a flourmill at Hungate on this date. He was on a gantry suspended from the ceiling, and had just loosened a wire rope attached to one of

the roof girders when it dropped and struck him, knocking him off the gantry and causing him to fall 19ft to the floor. When his co-workers arrived, they found that he was unable to move his legs and so they strapped him to a stretcher and proceeded to lower him eight storeys to the ground. This turned out to be a lengthy procedure, involving cutting through two of the floors of the building to provide access. Sadly, it was all to no avail, as he later died in hospital.

12 NOVEMBER 1864 Alice Wilson travelled from York to Howden on a carrier's cart on this date. On arrival in the small minster town, Alice told the carter that her mother lived in the town and that she would collect money for the fare. However, she absconded and travelled to nearby Booth, where her mother actually lived. She arrived there with her daughter, aged 3 years, but her mother was surprised that she did not have her 9-month-old baby son with her. A neighbour also enquired about the child, and in both cases Alice told them that the boy had died in the past week, while she had been in the workhouse in York, and had been buried. However, it transpired that she had been seen nursing the boy during the journey to Howden, and when pressed on the matter, would only say that the boy was buried 'under Sarah Long's pig-sty'. On her arrest she claimed to have accidentally smothered the child in a blanket during the journey, but she was found guilty of its murder and sentenced to death, although the sentence was later commuted.

13 NOVEMBER 1905 John Pinkney lived in Langwith Lane in Heslington, along with his wife and five children, and worked as a shepherd. The previous week he had been suspended from work for a few days, although later reinstated, and on this date Herbert Daniels, his insurance agent, came to the house to collect some money and found the house locked up and dark. This was unusual so, along with a neighbour, Daniels peered in through the kitchen window and saw what he thought to be a dead body. Fetching the police, they broke into the house and found Pinkney behind the door with his throat severely cut and a razor next to his hand. His wife was found next, severely battered and still breathing, although she expired within a few moments. Three of the five children were also dead, apparently beaten to death by their father with a bill hook, and a fourth, 6-year-old Arthur, was found huddled up to his mother's body with his face gashed open, his skull fractured and a thumb and finger severed. The final child, 4-year-old Eva, was in hospital at the time of the incident. From the state of dress of the victims, the police believed that the killings occurred while Pinkney's wife was preparing breakfast at around 7 a.m.

14 NOVEMBER 1884 The *Yorkshire Gazette* reported that at the York Assizes, 18-year-old Edward Fleming, from Skelton, was charged with a sexual assault on a 6-year-old girl by the name of Mary Andrews – his niece. The report states that he 'was visiting his sister's when the outrage was perpetrated, it being disclosed by the child being found to have contracted a loathsome disease'.

15 NOVEMBER 1919 Ralph Cuss was the landlord of the Garrick's Head Inn in Petergate, and had joined up with the army shortly after the beginning of the First World War in order to do his duty to King and Country. He had seen active duty in the trenches in France, and since his demobilisation and return, friends and relatives had found him a much-changed man, as is often the case with those who have been to war. He was often quiet and melancholy, and had the aspect of one who had seen too much suffering and death. On this date, at 9.45 a.m., he was on Platform 4 of York station, and as a train from the North began to pull into the station, he suddenly ran and jumped from the platform directly in front of the engine. The train was still travelling at enough speed that he was likely killed instantly. He left no note, or gave any indication that it was anything other than a spur-of-the-moment act.

The Garrick's Head in Petergate, early nineteenth century. (Author's collection)

16 NOVEMBER 1821 Workmen digging the foundations for three new houses on the corner of Micklegate and Barker's Lane on this date made a major discovery. From the depth of 2ft down to about 12ft, the ground was found to be a mass of human bones and deep black mould, clearly the site of a mass burial at some point in the past. Initial theories were that the bones were those of plague victims, or that the area was possibly the burial site of the Jews who had died in the massacre of 1190. Another theory was that it was the site of the cemetery from the lost church of St Gregory. However, as the workmen sifted through the remains, they found a red clay sacramental urn and Roman coins, and as the old road leading out of the Roman

camp would have passed very close by, it was generally accepted that the bones dated from that time, although experts were unable to identify at what point during the 300 years of Roman occupation they would have been deposited there.

Roman stone coffins, excavated in York and now on display in the Museum Gardens. (Author's collection)

17 NOVEMBER 1866 Three days of heavy rains led to widespread flooding across Yorkshire and Lancashire on this day, believed to be some of the worst ever seen in the district. The River Ouse was said to have raised its level by some 15ft, which had caused it to burst its banks and spread through the cellars of the city. At Aldwark, near Boroughbridge, the waters swept away the wooden central span of a viaduct, and the debris swept into the city, smashing into boats and the pillars of the Ouse Bridge and causing extensive damage. It was said that the bodies of sheep that had not been moved to higher land quickly enough also came floating down through the city, and these had to be cleared as a matter of urgency for fear that disease would fester in the corpses.

18 NOVEMBER 1883 A York city councilman by the name of Leak was found hanged in his bedroom on this morning. Leak was a druggist by trade and kept a small store in Walmgate, where he left his assistant in charge while he went to his private residence above the shop, saying he needed to make his daily toilet. However, when he did not come back down, his assistant became alarmed. His fears only grew when he found the bedroom locked and no answer from within. He obtained assistance from two policemen who were nearby and together they broke down the door and discovered Mr Leak's lifeless body. When found, he was naked and had prepared himself a bath. He had been seeking treatment for depression, but otherwise no motive was discovered.

19 NOVEMBER 1797 A strange case came up at the York Assizes of two highwaymen who resided in York. George Ledger was a shoemaker who kept a shop at the bottom of the Shambles, and Robert Hollingsworth was a general labourer. The two men both hailed from Rotherham but were not known to be acquaintances, and it was said that they never socialised, nor was Hollingsworth ever seen in Ledger's shop. At night, however, they would ride out together and lay in wait for folk leaving the city from the markets after the hours of darkness. Their downfall came on this date when they attempted to rob a man named William Nicholson, who put up stout resistance. During the struggle

The Shambles, *c.* 1900. (Author's collection)

Nicholson's hat came off, as did that of Hollingsworth, and each man then picked up the wrong hat. When Nicholson realised what had happened, he handed the hat over to the authorities who traced the hatmaker, and from there its owner. Thinking it might help him escape the noose, Hollingsworth then implicated Ledger in the crime. However, in this he was unsuccessful, as both men were hanged on 7 April of the following year.

20 NOVEMBER 1874 A Mr Oakley, a native of Rugby but working at Birdsall Hall to the East of York, was returning from some entertainment on this night in a horse and buggy in the company of his sweetheart, a village schoolmistress, as well as a Mrs Cameron and her child. As they travelled down a lane they turned at a corner where a post had been put up to protect the footpath. The wheel of the cart struck the post, overturning the vehicle. The two women and the child were thrown free, one of them suffering a serious injury from which she recovered, but Oakley went over with the cart, which came down on top of him as his head struck the ground, causing a fracturing of his skull. He died in the hospital a few hours afterwards.

21 NOVEMBER 1860 James Cobley was a well-known face around York, coming to the city regularly to attend horse fairs in his capacity as a horse dealer's assistant. He always stayed with a Mrs Webster who kept a house just outside the Micklegate Bar, and had been a regular guest for over twenty years. However, when he arrived on this date she found him in distress, saying he had had no food in days, and that due to rheumatism he was no longer able to work. Having been discharged from hospital in Hull, he hadn't known what to do and so had travelled to York to see if he could find any help there. Mrs Webster gave him lodging and food for a few days, then suggested he go to the workhouse, but having always been a hard-working man of means, he had never had any dealings with such a place and had no idea how to go about it. On the next day he was seen by several people at various places around the town, but on the Sunday evening his body was found on the railway lines just outside the bar walls. In his notebook he had written down details of his name and date of birth along with the words, 'age, pain, poverty and starvation have overtaken me, I fear it's more than I can stand'. The coroner concluded that he had thrown himself from the city wall, landing on the tracks.

22 NOVEMBER 1225 A set of accounts written around this date by Eustace of Lowdham, at the time the Sheriff of Yorkshire, records the expense of 2*s* for 'a chain

to hang Robert of Wetherby'. Little is known of Wetherby himself, except that he was an outlaw of some description, and that no little expense was spent on his capture, the exchequer having earlier that year granted Eustace 40s to be spent on an operation to 'seek and take and behead Robert of Wetherby, outlaw and evildoer of our land'. Another 28s for a similar purpose was spent the following year on the expenses of his execution. All of this suggests that he was captured and hanged, most likely in York, given the involvement of the sheriff and the proximity of Wetherby. Many historians now believe Robert of Wetherby to have been the historical character around whom the stories of Robin Hood were founded.

23 NOVEMBER 1820 While heading for the Barrack Tavern on the New Walk on this night, John Armstrong was approached by two men, who came across the Blue Bridge. One of the men, William Brown, grabbed him by the collar and demanded money. When he refused, Brown struck him six or seven times with a hefty stick, knocking him to the ground and then climbed on to his chest, pinning him to the ground. He searched Armstrong's pockets and came up with 16s and a promissory note. Then Brown and his accomplice lifted Armstrong and threw him over the bridge into the River Foss. By luck, Armstrong managed to cling to a post rising out of the river and cried out for assistance until three men happened along and managed to drag him out of the water. Armstrong knew Brown, as did one of the men who had assisted him, who also saw Brown fleeing the scene. Brown was hanged at York City Gaol on 14 April 1821, the second of two men hanged that day. His accomplice was not identified.

24 NOVEMBER 1906 A dense fog shrouded the York area on this night when the Scarborough to Leeds express train left York station a few minutes late at just after 7 p.m. There was also a goods train carrying minerals on the same line, and the intention was to stop that train on the main line, while the passenger train was switched to a parallel line to pass it before moving back on to the main line. This required the passenger train to be stopped briefly at Bolton Percy, just outside the city, but although three signals were set, the driver, John Dunham, must have failed to see them through the fog as the express, picking up speed and travelling at around 50mph, ploughed into the back of the other train. The engine and rear car of the goods train were completely wrecked, and the first two carriages of the passenger train derailed although without loss of life. However, the driver and his fireman Edward Booth were trapped in the burning wreckage of the engine and were found to have burned to death.

The aftermath of the rail crash of 24 November 1906. (Author's collection)

25 NOVEMBER 1582 James Thompson was born into a wealthy family in York, and as a young man travelled overseas to attend college in Reims, in France. Arriving in September 1580, he attended the college until the following May, when he enrolled at a Catholic seminary in Soissons. Twelve days later he was ordained as a priest, and in August was sent back to York. This was during the suppression of the Catholic faith under new laws passed by Elizabeth I, and a year later Thompson was arrested and taken before the Council of the North where he openly confessed his faith. Those who knew him expressed astonishment, as he had been brought up in a good Protestant family and had been away for less than a year. On this date he was taken before the court at York Castle and sentenced to death; he was hanged three days later at the Knavesmire. In his final speech he stated that he died in the Catholic faith but that he had never plotted against the queen. Whilst hanging he is said to have raised his hands to heaven, placed his right hand over his heart, and then made the sign of the cross before he died.

26 NOVEMBER 1585 Another priest who suffered under Elizabeth's suppression was Hugh Taylor, but in this case he was not alone in his fate. Marmaduke Bowes was the owner of the estate of Angram Grange, near Appleton in Cleveland, and was a secret follower of the Catholic faith while keeping up the outward appearance of a Protestant. He used his position to help Catholic priests to move around the country, allowing them to stay on his property in secret. Naturally members of his household were aware of this and, when his children's former tutor was arrested and about to be arraigned at York Castle, the tutor became aware that Hugh Taylor was under arrest there on charges of being a priest, and recognised the man as one of those his former employer had aided. In order to prevent his own prosecution, he agreed to give evidence against both Taylor and Bowes, and accordingly the two men were executed on this date.

27 NOVEMBER 1882 On this date a fisherman named Edward Wheatfill was put to death by hanging at York Castle for the murder of a young hand on his fishing boat. Peter Hughes had been 16 years old when he put to sea on the fishing boat *Gleaner*, on which Wheatfill was the second mate. For some reason, the older man seemed to take delight in torturing the boy, tormenting him almost daily by forcing him to carry out duties on deck naked in all weathers, as well as gutting fish in the ice room in the same state of undress. On 22 February, Hughes accidentally set fire to part of the boat with a paraffin fog signal he had been making, and as a result Wheatfill had kicked him wearing heavy boots for forty-five minutes, resulting in much of the flesh of his hands being torn off as he tried to protect his face. Two days later, at around 4 a.m., the two were on deck together when a scuffle was heard from below, and then Wheatfill appeared and told the crew that Hughes had fallen overboard and was lost.

28 NOVEMBER 1724 On this date, York saw the appointment of a new archbishop: Lancelot Blackburne. There is nothing specifically unusual about this appointment, except that Blackburne himself had a reputation as a somewhat colourful character. Graduating from Christ Church, Oxford in 1680, he had travelled to the West Indies, where he spent four years in and around the island of Nevis. In 1681, there is a record of his receiving £20 from Charles II for 'secret services'. Although not confirmed, it was strongly rumoured that he spent those years as a pirate, and that his service to the king had been in attacking Spanish ships. He later became a personal chaplain to George I and is rumoured to have conducted a secret marriage service between the king and his mistress. Although married himself, he also had a married mistress: a Mrs Conwys, whom he later moved into his own marital home along with his wife. He seems to have lived a most irreligious life, indulging in carnal pleasures whenever the opportunity arose, and in one famous incident was ejected from a church after asking for his pipe, tobacco and ale to be brought to him during a service.

29 NOVEMBER 1886 When James Murphy of Barnsley was arrested for drunkenness by Police Constable Alfred Austwick and later fined, he told friends that he would one day have vengeance on the policeman. Four months later, Austwick was called to a disturbance in a house in Dodworth and Murphy answered the door. Saying to the constable, 'You're just the one I want,' Murphy went into the house, collected his shotgun, and shot the officer dead on the doorstep. He was hanged on this date at York Castle, the only hanging there to be conducted by the famous hangman James Berry. Murphy seems to have been entirely sanguine to the results of his crime. Meeting Berry for the first time he told him, 'I won't give you any trouble,' and made a joke about being 'hanged' if he knew what all the fuss was about.

30 NOVEMBER 1894 John Battle lived in Hope Street and worked in the city as a labourer. To make ends meet he rented out his spare room to an Italian gentleman named Giovanni Valente, who busked in the streets as an organ grinder. Valente was in the habit of keeping his organ within the house, where it often got in Battle's way, and so he asked his lodger to store it somewhere else. At this, Valente flew into a rage, leapt from his seat and struck Battle across the back of his neck with an open razor, causing a deep and severe wound. Valente then ran from the house and was not seen again. Battle was taken to the hospital in a serious condition, but eventually recovered.

DECEMBER

View of the minster from the city walls. (Author's collection)

1 DECEMBER 1751 An unnamed woman from the countryside around York had some business in the city, and managed to hitch a ride on a cart carrying milk from a nearby dairy farm. The woman sat on the rear of the cart, taking up a space between two large milk cans and fairly wedged between them. As the cart was approaching a busy area near the city another cart, heavily loaded with goods, jostled the one on which she was riding, causing the milk cans to topple off the cart, taking her with them. As she fell to the ground the second cart, unable to stop, ran its wheels over her legs, breaking both of them in several places. She was taken to York County Hospital, where it was said she was lucky to survive.

2 DECEMBER 1890 Workers were busy going about their daily duties at Kirk's Glass Works on Peasholm Green on this day when Edward Kemp, the brother of the proprietor of the business, climbed the ladder to the manhole of the furnace to make a manual check on progress. Nobody paid much attention to this, until they realised that he had been up there an awfully long time. They shouted up to him but receiving no answer, somebody climbed up and found that he was quite dead. Apparently, having opened the manhole cover, he had been overcome by the fumes and suffocated to death.

3 DECEMBER 1745 Throughout the previous month York had been bracing itself as the rebel army of the Jacobites, under the command of Charles Edward Stewart (also known as 'Bonnie Prince Charlie'), had swept down through the country from Edinburgh, defeating all who stood in their path. However, to the citizens' relief, the army had seemed to sidestep York and move south through Penrith. On this date, eleven members of that army arrived in York Castle under arrest, the first to be so taken. Ten had been taken at Lowther Hall in Westmoreland, after the steward of Lord Lonidale had roused the neighbourhood and a short gun battle had ensued.

4 DECEMBER 1865 An inquest held in York into the death of William Davies concluded that death had been accidental, due to a mix-up regarding two bottles. Mr Davies had been in poor health and had been in the habit of taking chloric ether as a medicine to help him sleep at nights. As a result, he had a tendency to sleep quite late, and so nobody was surprised when he didn't rise early in the morning, but by 10 a.m. the staff had become worried and, going to his room, found him in a state of deep unconsciousness. Next to his bed was a bottle the same size and shape as that of the remedy he usually administered, but it contained chloroform. As the two liquids smelled almost identical, it was concluded that in a tired state he had picked up the wrong one and had poisoned himself accordingly. He never recovered consciousness and died around three hours after the discovery.

5 DECEMBER 1730   When Charles Bathurst, former Sheriff of York, offered his house guest Mr Motley a horn of beer, few would have expected that things could get so out of hand. Motley was not inclined to take a drink and said so, whereupon Bathurst became offended at this refusal of hospitality, and during the ensuing argument went to fetch his sword. Discretion being the better part of valour, Motley chose to quickly leave and Bathurst ordered the doors locked against him; there should have been an end to the matter. Later, while half undressed and readying himself for bed, Bathurst heard voices in the kitchen and thought it might be Motley. Taking up the sword again he headed downstairs, telling another servant that if Motley had returned, he would force him to drink the beer. However, instead he found his butler, who had apparently drunk the beer himself and was now brandishing a red-hot poker recently taken out of the kitchen fire and seemed enraged at Bathurst's treatment of Motley. The butler pushed twice at Bathurst with the poker, forcing him backwards, and on the second occasion, with his back against the wall, his master thrust out with the sword, killing him on the spot.

6 DECEMBER 1801   When Thomas Taylor of Elvington and his family arose for their breakfast, Mrs Taylor went out to the pump to fill the kettle and noticed that the water was slightly cloudy. However, this was not vastly out of the ordinary so she thought no more about it until the family had drunk their tea and started to experience extreme nausea and sickness. The pump was examined, and it was discovered that a white powder had been smeared on the inside of the pipe, which was found to be arsenic. Doctors were called and managed to attend to the family without fatality, and Taylor published an advertisement in the newspapers offering a reward of 50 guineas to anyone who could shed light on the matter, but it remained a mystery.

7 DECEMBER 1892   In the very early hours, James English, a guard on the North Eastern Railroad, was seen leaving the Coach and Horses Inn in Micklegate and heading towards Lower Priory Street. He was not seen again until almost a year later, on the afternoon of 11 November, when some men operating a dredger on the River Ouse found that one of their sand buckets had become entangled. Drawing it up, they found that a body had been pulled up from the riverbed. It was said to be in a badly decomposed state and quite gruesome to look at. A piece of paper in one of

the pockets of the man's clothing revealed the word 'English', leading to the suspicion that this was the body of the missing man. His daughter later identified his pocket watch to put the matter beyond doubt.

8 DECEMBER 1882 When William Archer and Annie Emmitt checked in to the lodging house of Mr Morgan of Tanner's Row a few days before this date, the proprietor accepted their explanation that they were a newly wedded couple. Despite their age, Archer being 18 and Emmitt a year younger, they seemed like a pleasant honeymooning couple. They stayed for two days and then returned for a third night, saying they had meant to walk to Hopgrove but been caught in a storm. The following morning, on this date, the waiting maid of the establishment was shocked to find Emmitt standing on the landing with blood pouring from a throat wound. Archer was found to have securely locked the door to their room, so a policeman was called. He broke in and found that the young man had tried to take his own life also by cutting his throat. Both were attended and survived, and it was discovered that the pair had eloped, having become intimate after working nearby each other at Oswaldkirk. Archer's defence was that he claimed to have no memory of harming the girl, and on discovering he had done so he had attempted to end his own life in distress. He was sentenced to four months' hard labour.

9 DECEMBER 1895 Frank Ramsden, 18, had recently been reading some books about gunfights, and decided it might be exciting to own a gun of his own. He went out and bought one and showed it to lots of people, including his colleague William Lawson, who also lodged with his family, sleeping in the same bed. On this morning, Ramsden told Lawson he was taking the gun to their place of work, and Lawson asked him not to. During the day, he continued to show his gun to many people, and as they were nearing the end of the working day, Ramsden pulled a cartridge from a pouch on his belt, loaded it into the gun and pointed it at Lawson's head. The gun went off, although Ramsden swore he had never intended it to. Luckily, Lawson had heard the clicks as the gun cocked and started to duck, and as a result the bullet hit his skull at an angle and was deflected away. Doctors who examined the wound stated that if the angle of the weapon had been two-fifths of an inch lower, the bullet would have smashed through the skull and entered the brain, almost certainly killing him.

10 DECEMBER 1846 On this day the Northern Circuit Court in York heard the rather shocking story of a young lad attempting to poison an entire family. George Adamson, 16 years of age, was apprenticed to a man named Alfred Bramah, a tailor and draper, and lived with his family. On the night in question, Mr Bramah had gone out to a lecture while his wife was making porridge for supper. She left the kitchen twice during that time: once to buy some treacle, and the other to attend to something upstairs. Adamson was said to be engaged in emptying the fireplace at this time, and it is suggested that on one of these occasions he took the opportunity of her absence to add poison to the saucepan. As the meal neared readiness he loudly announced twice that he would want very little supper as he had eaten an apple and was given only a small plate, which he barely touched. He then went to bed and shortly afterwards the rest of the family became violently ill and experienced burning sensations in the throat. A doctor was called who managed to apply an emetic, which relieved all but Mrs Bramah, whose stomach was pumped. The contents of her stomach showed the presence of white arsenic. The boy eventually confessed, giving as his motive only that 'the devil must have got into me'.

11 DECEMBER 1883 An Irish labourer by the name of Martin Kevill murdered his 7-year-old son in Hope Street on this date by chopping off his head with a hatchet. The night before, Kevill had argued with his wife and thrown her out of the house, and at 7 a.m. the next day he took his son out of bed and carried out the horrible deed. Medical practitioners testified at his trial that he almost certainly had some kind of brain injury as a result of falling off a ladder two years earlier, and that his mind was unbalanced at the time of the killing. The jury at his trial found him guilty of murder, but mitigated by his mental instability. He was therefore sentenced to be detained at an asylum during Her Majesty's pleasure.

12 DECEMBER 1892 The city coroner held inquests on this date on two separate instances of death by fire. In the first, James Gawthorpe stated that he had gone to bed in the house that he shared with his mother, Mary, in Cemetery Road, and had later heard her coming up to bed herself when she gave a shout. He jumped up and found that the wood of one of the stairs had rotted. As she had climbed them her foot had gone through, resulting in her dropping the lamp she was carrying and setting her clothes on fire. She was admitted to the hospital and died from her burns around a week later. In the other incident, that of 6-year-old Mary Ann Sissions, her mother had left her playing in the house with other children while she attended to something in the yard. One of the other children said that they had been playing with a piece of paper on the hearth of the fire, which had no guard, and her pinafore had caught fire. Her mother stated that she had not been out of the room more than two minutes when the incident occurred. Both incidents were recorded as verdicts of accidental death.

13 DECEMBER 1856 Strange scenes occurred in the courtroom at York Castle on this date as a man named John Hannah was convicted of the murder of Jane Banham, an Australian woman with whom he had been cohabiting at Armley, near Leeds, and had two children. Banham had left him and he had gone to a public house to try and win her back, but on taking her into a back room, the other customers heard screams and rushed into the room to find him cutting her throat with a razor. As they tried to tend to her wound, he had apparently placed a cap on his head and said, 'I am done with her now, they can do as they like with me.' At the subsequent trial he was said to have been in a horrendous state, looking drawn and haggard and far older than his 22 years. On being asked to plead he had burst into tears and been hardly able to speak, and for most of the trial he shook so violently that he was barely able to stand. When the sentence of death was passed against him, he simply fainted on the spot.

York Crown Court, formerly the Assizes Court. (Author's collection)

14 DECEMBER 2004 Between 2004 and 2005, York Archaeological Trust undertook excavations in Driffield Terrace and made something of a startling discovery. What they found appeared to be a burial ground dating from Roman times, in which they found some eighty bodies, the majority of which appeared to have

A pillar from the Great Hall of the Roman fortress. (Author's collection)

died violently. The bodies were mostly taller and more heavily built than the average Roman, and many had not merely fatal wounds, but also evidence of older wounds that had healed. Comparing these bodies to other similar finds, the evidence pointed to the likelihood that they had been gladiators. Some of the bodies had been buried with trinkets that would have been won for fighting bravely, several appeared to have been decapitated or died as a result of hammer blows to the head, and at least one had suffered a bite from a tiger. While it had long been suspected that the Roman city had an amphitheatre for gladiatorial combat, this has never been confirmed, and the location, if it existed, is not known.

15 DECEMBER 1890 In a feature on the twenty-fourth anniversary of the Oaks Colliery mining disaster, the worst in UK history which had occurred near Barnsley, the *Yorkshire Evening Post* of this date published an excerpt from a letter from Lord Houghton to his wife, in which he recounted his trip from York to visit the site in company with the archbishop. He wrote that when one man, 'saved as by a miracle, was taken home, his wife burst out in abuse of the people who brought him for not leaving him in the pit, saying he was such a blackguard, and she had hoped she was shut of him.'

16 DECEMBER 1943 During a concerted Allied effort to raid Berlin, 498 aircraft took part in the mission that was undertaken on this night. Many of these operated out of the Linton-on-Ouse airfield near York. The raid was successful, but on their return, adverse weather conditions had caused a thick blanket of fog to cover the entire York area and the aircraft were having trouble landing. Several ran out of fuel in the air, and one of these, a Lancaster bomber circling to find the airfield, ended up crashing on Murton Common in the Osbaldwick district of the city. Most of the crew were killed, but two survived the crash. Two other Lancasters from the base also crashed; one near Knaresborough and the other just outside Thirsk.

17 DECEMBER 1839 Samuel Holgate, one of the senior prison officers at York Castle, received information on this date of the whereabouts of a man named William Sellers and, travelling to the East Riding, apprehended him in the home of a distant relative. Sellers, who had been sentenced to life imprisonment for the murder of his mother, had escaped from his cell nearly a month earlier in the company of two other men. One of them, James Coates, had been a locksmith prior to his incarceration and had managed to manufacture duplicate keys to aid their escape; they had also used torn up rugs to make ropes with which to scale the walls. Coates had been sentenced to seven years' transportation for larceny, but had remained in York for the previous three years by volunteering as hangman at the prison, during which time he had carried out a number of hangings. The third man, William Marshall, was also serving a life sentence for murder, and he had already been apprehended. Coates was never heard from again.

18 DECEMBER 1912 An inquest was held in York into the death of Hannah Dutton, who was found hanging from a bedpost in the house of her cousin, John Dutton, in Russell Street. Ms Dutton had been in service with a woman named Hopkinson in St Mary's in the city until six weeks before, when her mistress had died. With no work, being of advanced years with no husband to support her and having little prospect of finding a new position, she had thrown herself on the charity of her family and had been staying at her cousin's house ever since. However, it seemed that she had become greatly depressed with her situation, feeling that she could impose on the family no more, and decided that suicide was the only way out of her predicament.

19 DECEMBER 1824 Robert Manners left Pocklington, near York, heading for Beverley on this date. A young man by the name of Richard Holderness rode along with him, and he encountered the man again on the return journey, at the village of Bishop Barton. About a mile and a half further along the road, Holderness caught up with his cart and joined him again on the journey. As they travelled, Manners put his head down for a rest, knowing that his horses would stick to the road. As he lay there he experienced a sudden pain in the head and felt his mouth fill with blood. Holderness leapt from the cart shouting, 'damn those villains, they have nearly pulled my legs off'. Manners observed that Holderness was reloading a pistol and realised the other man had shot him, so pulled on the reigns and got the horses moving at full trot. The pistol was later found in a bush near to where the incident occurred, and a doctor, tracing the wound, showed that it had to have been fired at almost point-blank range. Holderness later confessed to the crime, and when asked if he was trying to rob Manners replied that he was not, but had held a grudge against him for an old quarrel. He was hanged for attempted murder the following year.

20 DECEMBER 1853 John Hall, a businessman from Scarborough, had come to York to attend the great Christmas horse show. He had a few too many drinks and managed to fall in with a pair of young prostitutes named Isabella Campbell and Caroline Nicholson. Having ascertained that he had £50 in cash about his person, the pair took him down to King's Staith, where they intended to rob him. However, in his intoxicated state, he tripped and fell into the River Ouse as they pushed him about. A man named Sargent, who was passing, attempted to reach him with an oar, but Hall

was unable to keep himself above water and was last seen disappearing beneath the hull of a boat. The river was dragged for two hours before his body was found.

21 DECEMBER 1887 Several newspapers reported on a Herbert Culling, a member of the 'Man to Man' theatre company who had recently been playing at York's Theatre Royal, and had been arrested at that time for stealing property from the company. He had since been held in York Castle where, a few days previous, he had attempted to strangle himself with his own bootlace. After recovering, he asked to speak to the governor and stated that his reason for attempting suicide was the guilt he felt over the murder of a sailor in Oldham, who he had shot in a quarrel over a card game and then had buried in a field along with another man. Enquiries were made, but nobody in the area remembered any of the events he described, and the field in which he claimed he had buried the man was dug up, but no body found. The general opinion was that he had made the story up to get out of hard labour detail.

22 DECEMBER 1829 On this night, three men called at a shop run by a Mrs Whitehead on Walmgate and asked if she could point them to where they could gain lodging. They explained that they had been unsuccessful in the place across the street and asked her if there might be somewhere further away. She directed them to an establishment in Paver's Lane but, when she tried to give directions, they made as if not to understand. Eventually she offered that her son, who was 10 years old, would show them the way. The boy was sent on the errand and, on arriving at the other location, the men suddenly seized him and slapped a tar plaster on his face that covered his nose and mouth, making it impossible to breathe. By providence, a girl was in a dark stairway across the road and spotted this: she ran out, shouting at the men, who fled, and she tore off the plaster, allowing the boy to recover. The men were spotted again the next day and were said to have left town on the Hull Road. It was suggested that the men had been inspired by the recent case of Burke and Hare, who sold the bodies of their murder victims to the medical schools, as the tar plaster would have been a successful way of killing the boy without leaving marks of violence.

23 DECEMBER 1847 A shocking murder case from Leeds came to a dramatic conclusion on this date at York Castle. Michael McCabe, an Irish hawker, had knocked on the door of James Wraith's house in Leeds on 12 May of that year and asked the person who answered if he would like to buy anything from his cart. Although the man closed the door quickly, McCabe noticed blood on the floor and heard muffled groans. However, there being anti-Irish sentiment at the time, he decided to say nothing in case he came under suspicion himself. Later that day, Wraith's nephew called at the house and found his uncle's lifeless body lying in a pool of blood with his throat cut. Wraith's wife Ann was nearby with a fractured skull and her right eye gouged out. The couple's servant, Caroline Ellis, was also found dead, with her brains dashed out. When word got out about the murder, McCabe, by now drunk, mentioned to someone what he had seen and that he had recognised the person who answered the door as a fellow Irish tinker, Patrick Reid. He and Reid were both arrested, and the police, coming to the conclusion that they had acted together, put them both on trial. Initially tried at York on 19 June, the testimony was so confusing that the jury could reach no conclusion, and they had to be retried on 20 December, whereupon both were found guilty and sentenced to death. Immediately following sentence, Reid's attorney produced a signed confession from his client exonerating McCabe entirely, which he had held in his pocket throughout both trials but had not revealed. A reprieve for McCabe was quickly requested from the Home Secretary and received on this date. Reid was executed on 8 January 1848.

24 DECEMBER 1944 The V1 flying bomb was one of the deadliest weapons in the German arsenal during the Second World War, but with a flying range of only 150 miles, nobody expected to see them over northern England. However, in an attempt to attack Manchester, the Luftwaffe adapted a squadron of Heinkel 111 aircraft to each carry a single V1 across the North Sea and release them over Hull to travel the rest of the way by themselves. The raid took place on the morning of Christmas Eve and, at 5.50 a.m., the peace of the quiet village of Barmby Moor was disturbed by a huge explosion that shook the houses, causing damage to several. One of the V1s had veered off course and come down just outside the village, close to the RAF base at Elvington. Miraculously, nobody was killed, although a Halifax bomber aircraft at the base was badly damaged. A large pond that now stands on the outskirts of the village is, in fact, the crater created by the explosion.

25 DECEMBER 1069 William the Conqueror is said to have celebrated the Nativity in York this year, having marched north to put an end to what had been a tempestuous few months. Edgar Aetheling, who had been proclaimed as the English king on the death of Harold at Hastings but never crowned, had been for some time in exile in Scotland, but had marched south with the support of his new brother-in-law, the Scottish King Malcolm Canmore. Joining up with Northumbrian rebels and the army of King Sweyn Estrithson of Denmark, Edgar had invaded York, as described in the entry for 19 September. Partly in retribution, and partly to prevent Edgar's armies from being able to locate supplies

should they invade again, William instigated what would become known as the Harrying of the North. He ordered his troops to cover an area from the Humber to the Tees, where their instructions were to burn down all the villages, kill all the livestock, destroy the crops, and salt the ground so that nothing could grow. The Norman monk Orderic Vitalis described the event thus: 'In his anger he commanded that all crops and herds, chattels and food of every kind be brought together and burned to ashes with consuming fire, so that the whole region north of the Humber might be stripped of all means of sustenance.' Another contemporary chronicler, Simeon of Durham, wrote: 'There was such hunger that men ate the flesh of their own kind, of horses and dogs and cats. Others sold themselves into perpetual slavery that they might be able to sustain their miserable lives. It was horrible to look into the ruined farmyards and houses and see the human corpses dissolved into corruption, for there were none to bury them for all were gone either in flight, or cut down by the sword and famine.' In total, around 100,000 were said to have perished in the act. Orderic finished his account, 'I have often praised William, but I can say nothing good about this brutal slaughter. God will punish him.'

26 DECEMBER 1851 Elizabeth Bradley gave birth to a child, George, at the workhouse in Malton, near York, on this date. Sadly, George was destined to have a short and unpleasant life. Other inmates regularly heard Elizabeth complaining about the child and she was said to have treated him badly and regularly left him without food, causing him to suffer from convulsions. During one of these occurrences it was found that the mother had tied his genitals so tightly as to prevent urination. Bradley regularly told people that she wished the child was dead so she could leave the workhouse, and later told another inmate that she had knocked the boy's head on the door knob and on a bedpost in order to try to kill him. In May of that year, she got her wish: the workhouse doctor found the child in a state of stupor and two days later, George died. The mother confessed that she had hit the boy's head on a wall to cause this. She was sent to York to stand trial, but the grand jury threw the case out because the only evidence against her was the confession and she was considered not in a sound state of mind when she made it.

27 DECEMBER 1874 A case came up on this date against William Scholefield for an assault on one Solomon Kirk at Gate Fulford. The incident had happened a week before when Kirk, leaving the Saddle public house in the town, had been set upon while drunk. He was so badly injured in this attack that at this point it was unsure whether he would die, and so the magistrate adjourned the hearing at the York Castle, moving the venue to the victim's bedside so that he could testify. He could remember little of the

incident, but others stated that Kirk had been sparring in a friendly way with a man named Scarth when Scholefield and another man named Albert Thorpe set on him and beat him insensible. It transpired that Kirk and Thorpe had been arguing about wages in the public house and Kirk had offered to fight the man for a sovereign. Thorpe had since absconded and a warrant was now issued for his arrest. Eventually, Thorpe alone stood trial for the assault, Scholefield being discharged for want of evidence.

28 DECEMBER 1749 The George Inn in Coney Street was the most important coaching inn in York until its closure and demolition in 1867. On this night an altercation occurred in the kitchen of the inn between two young servants of around 15 or 16 years of age. What they argued over is not recorded, but Joseph Vicars became so incensed with his compatriot John Bower that he picked up a kitchen knife and stabbed the other lad in the stomach. Bower was rushed to the hospital but died a few days later from the wound. Vicars was committed to the Ouse Bridge Gaol to await trial.

29 DECEMBER 1774 Farmer John Cross was on his way to market in York from Barmby on this date when he noticed a riderless horse with saddle and bridle. He supposed it to belong to a nearby carter but found this not to be the case. The two men made a search, and in a nearby ditch they found Francis Smith, who had also been travelling to market in the city from Pocklington. Smith, a butcher, was lying in a ditch with his head battered to such an extent that the newspapers reported that Cross was able to insert his hand in the fracture in his skull. The man was alive, barely, but unable to speak or give information about his attacker, and he died before they could get him to a nearby house to receive medical attention. Smith was on his way to buy cattle and so it was supposed he had a great deal of money on his person. It was considered that his assailant was most likely acquainted with the man and knew this to be the case.

30 DECEMBER 1460 Despite the Wars of the Roses being a conflict between the houses of York and Lancaster, by the end of 1460, York was in the hands of Lancastrian forces. Richard of York and his allies had captured King Henry VI, who was being held prisoner in London, and Richard had been declared Protector of the Realm and thus de-facto ruler of the country. However Henry's wife, Margaret of Anjou, was gathering an army in the North and in Scotland, so Richard and his son Edmund marched north with their army to Sandal Castle. Believing he had the support of Lord Neville and his army, Richard met the Lancastrian army at Wakefield on this date. However, when Neville held his army back and failed to join the fight, Richard's army was routed and Richard and his son were both killed. His body was taken to Pontefract, but his

Micklegate Bar in the early nineteenth century, with its barbican intact. (Author's collection)

head was brought to York where, for the next year, it was displayed on a pike on the Micklegate Bar wearing a paper crown to show that he was only a paper ruler.

31 DECEMBER 1904 When Harry Hewitt arrived home at the house of his adopted parents, William and Isabella, he was met by Constable Southwood, who asked him what he wanted there. Hewitt replied that he was there just to look around. On giving his name, Southwood immediately took him into custody. Around midnight on the night before, William Metcalfe had left his job at the Royal Station Hotel and, while passing down Blossom Street, heard someone shout the words 'Oh, no, don't!' before seeing a man wearing a billycock hat come running out of a passage and away in the direction of the Micklegate. Metcalfe then informed the police and the following morning a Sergeant Bain visited the property and found that its occupants had been murdered. William had been beaten to death by ten or eleven blows from something heavy. Isabella had also been struck heavily, and stabbed twice in the neck. Some of Harry Hewitt's clothes were found to have blood on them, and a bloodstained knife and mallet were also found at the house. However, the evidence against Hewitt himself was said to be merely circumstantial, and although he stood trial for the murders, he was acquitted.

ABOUT THE AUTHOR

ALAN SHARP owns an historical tour-guiding business in York and regularly conducts large numbers of tourists around the city. He is also a stand-up comedian, performing on television and in some of the top comedy clubs in the country. He has a BA in English and Drama from University College, Dublin, and was a contestant on the 2012 season of *Mastermind*.

BIBLIOGRAPHY

Books

Brandon, Ed and David, *Curiosities of York* (Stroud: Amberley Books, 2011)
Drake, Francis, *Eboracum: or the History and Antiquities of the City of York* (London: William Bower, 1736)
Knipe, William, *Criminal Chronology of York Castle* (York: C.L. Burdekin, 1867)
Nuttgens, Patrick and John Shannon, *York ... the Continuing City* (York: Maxiprint, 2001)
Ottaway, Patrick, *Roman York* (Stroud: Tempus, 2004)
Palliser, D.M., *The Reformation in York, 1534–1553* (York: St Anthony's Press, 1971)
Palliser, D.M., *Medieval York: 600–1540* (Oxford: University Press, 2014)
Wade, Stephen, *Yorkshire Hangmen* (Barnsley: Wharncliffe Books, 2008)

Websites

British History Online – www.british-history.ac.uk
British Newspaper Archive – www.britishnewspaperarchive.co.uk
History of York – www.historyofyork.org.uk
PastSearch – www.pastsearch-archeo-history.co.uk

Also from The History Press
YORKSHIRE

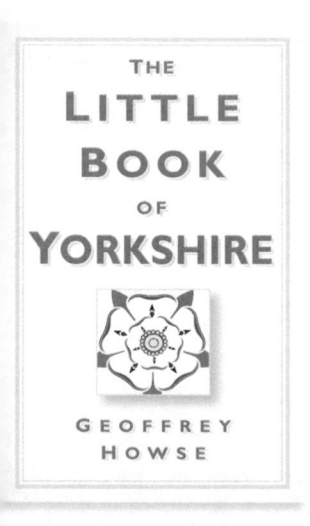

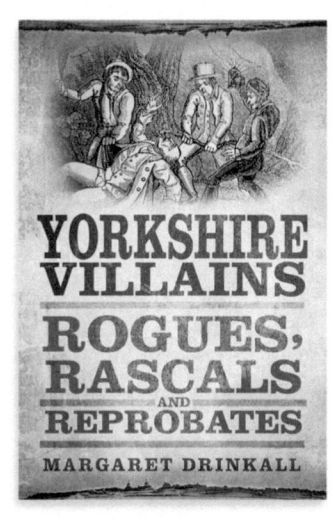

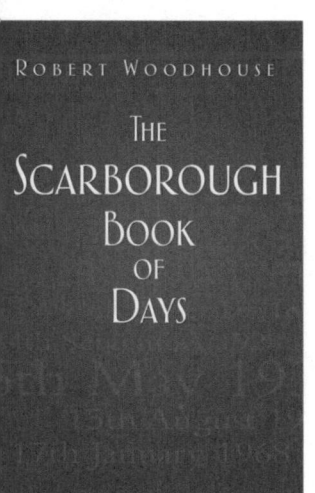

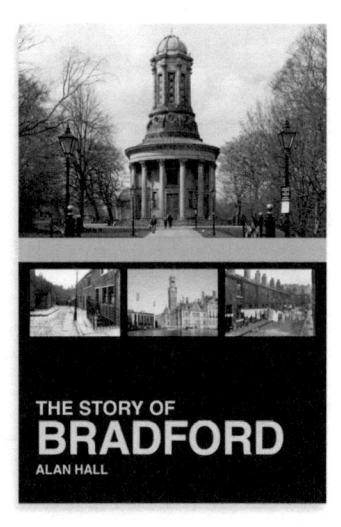

THE LITTLE BOOK OF YORKSHIRE
GEOFFREY HOWSE

YORK MURDER & CRIME
SUMMER STREVENS

YORKSHIRE VILLAINS ROGUES, RASCALS AND REPROBATES
MARGARET DRINKALL

ROBERT WOODHOUSE — THE SCARBOROUGH BOOK OF DAYS

BLOODY BRITISH HISTORY: LEEDS
RICHARD SMYTH

THE STORY OF BRADFORD
ALAN HALL

Find these titles and more at
www.thehistorypress.co.uk

The History Press